EDITH

MODERN SPIRITUAL MASTERS

Robert Ellsberg, Series Editor

This series introduces the writing and vision of some of the great spiritual masters of the twentieth century. Along with selections from their writings, each volume includes a comprehensive introduction, presenting the author's life and writings in context and drawing attention to points of special relevance to contemporary spirituality.

Some of these authors found a wide audience in their lifetimes. In other cases recognition has come long after their deaths. Some are rooted in long-established traditions of spirituality. Others charted new, untested paths. In each case, however, the authors in this series have engaged in a spiritual journey shaped by the influences and concerns of our age. Such concerns include the challenges of modern science, religious pluralism, secularism, and the quest for social justice.

At the dawn of a new millennium this series commends these modern spiritual masters, along with the saints and witnesses of previous centuries, as guides and companions to a new generation of seekers.

Already published:

Dietrich Bonhoeffer (edited by Robert Coles)
Simone Weil (edited by Eric O. Springsted)
Henri Nouwen (edited by Robert A. Jonas)
Pierre Teilhard de Chardin (edited by Ursula King)
Anthony de Mello (edited by William Dych, S.J.)
Charles de Foucauld (edited by Robert Ellsberg)
Oscar Romero (by Marie Dennis, Rennie Golden, and Scott Wright)
Eberhard Arnold (edited by Johann Christoph Arnold)
Thomas Merton (edited by Christine M. Bochen)
Thich Nhat Hanh (edited by Robert Ellsberg)
Rufus Jones (edited by Kerry Walters)
Mother Teresa (edited by Jean Maalouf)
John Main (edited by Lawrence Freeman)

Forthcoming volumes include:

Mohandas Gandhi
Flannery O'Connor
G. K. Chesterton

MODERN SPIRITUAL MASTERS SERIES

EDITH STEIN

(St. Teresa Benedicta of the Cross, O.C.D.)

Essential Writings

Selected
with an Introduction by
JOHN SULLIVAN, O.C.D.

ORBIS BOOKS
Maryknoll, New York 10545

Founded in 1970, Orbis Books endeavors to publish works that enlighten the mind, nourish the spirit, and challenge the conscience. The publishing arm of the Maryknoll Fathers and Brothers, Orbis seeks to explore the global dimensions of the Christian faith and mission, to invite dialogue with diverse cultures and religious traditions, and to serve the cause of reconciliation and peace. The books published reflect the views of their authors and do not represent the official position of the Maryknoll Society. To learn more about Maryknoll and Orbis Books, please visit our website at www.maryknoll.org.

Published by Orbis Books, Maryknoll, NY 10545-0308

Note to the reader: Apart from "The Prayer of the Church," "Holy Discretion in Spiritual Guidance," and "The Significance of Woman's Intrinsic Value in National Life" the selections in this book were excerpted from longer texts and may represent only a small part of the original.

For more information about St. Teresa Benedicta/Edith Stein and her works please visit the website of the Discalced Carmelites at www.icspublications.org.

Manufactured in the United States of America

Library of Congress Cataloging-in-Publication Data

Stein, Edith, Saint, 1891-1942.
[Selections. English. 2002]
Edith Stein : essential writings / selected with an introduction by John Sullivan.
p. cm. – (Modern spiritual masters series)
ISBN 1-57075-428-4 (pbk.)
1. Spiritual life – Catholic Church. 2. Catholic Church – Doctrines. 3. Stein, Edith, Saint, 1891-1942. I. Sullivan, John, 1942- II. Title. III. Series.
BX4705.S814 A25 2002
230′.2 – dc21

2001056110

To Rosa Stein
and
those who suffered
with her,
lest we forget.

Contents

Preface

The following selected passages from the writings of Edith Stein, or [St.] Teresa Benedicta of the Cross (her religious name), can only begin to convey the depth and significance of her life and its meaning today. Throughout several quite distinct phases of her rich life — as atheistic philosopher, lay Catholic educator, then dedicated Carmelite nun — she established a running dialogue with her contemporary world at a time of extraordinary intellectual and moral challenge. The following selections give a modest hint at the voice she raised, always positive and hopeful in her interactions both with groups and individuals. Soon after her canonization in 1998 there began to be talk that she might be proclaimed a Doctor of the Church. The texts chosen could very well warm the reader to that possibility.

The five chapters of this book reflect the major axes of what she did and propounded in her truncated life. The reader will detect subthemes that articulate concerns for which Edith Stein was well known, and which reflect the many facets of her personality and her vision. For any lacunae that result from my choices as compiler, I can only invoke a wonderfully humane one-liner she left us, "Be patient with yourself; God is."

A further word or two about other editorial options found in this compilation: In some instances slight variations in punctuation seemed useful, given the fact that most texts appear apart from the longer work in which they originally appeared. Only on a very rare occasion did I think it justified to change a word or phrase translated from German by the capable translators of the Collected Works of Edith Stein. Seasoned author that she was, of both scholarly and popular texts, St. Edith most likely would go along with such editorial choices.

Chronology

1891	Born into a Jewish family in Breslau, Prussia.
1911–13	University studies in Breslau (German history, psychology, philosophy; early part of atheistic phase).
1913–15	Philosophical studies in Göttingen under Edmund Husserl.
1915	Work as Red Cross volunteer.
1916	Passes doctoral exam *summa cum laude*.
1916–18	Assistant to Husserl in Freiburg.
1919–23	Private philosophical work; unsuccessful attempts to gain university position.
1922	Baptism, First Communion, Confirmation.
1923–31	Instructor at Teachers' College, Speyer.
1928–32	Public lectures, translations, and other work.
1932–33	Lecturer at German Institute for Scientific Pedagogy in Münster.
1933–38	Enters and receives formation in Cologne Carmel (Sr. Teresia Benedicta a Cruce).
1938	Final profession of vows.
1939–42	Stays at Echt Carmel, Netherlands; continues writing.
1942	Arrest, deportation, and death at Auschwitz/Birkenau.

1987	May 1. Beatification in Cologne, Germany.
1998	October 11. Canonization in St. Peter's Square, Rome.
1999	October 1. Declared co-patroness of Europe with St. Bridget of Sweden and St. Catherine of Siena.

Sources

CC Baird, Sr. M. Julian, R.S.M. "Edith Stein and the Mother of God," *Cross and Crown* 8 (1956): 423–24.

EW *Essays on Woman.* Translation of *Die Frau.* Translated by Freda Mary Oben. Collected Works of Edith Stein 2. Washington, D.C.: ICS Publications, 1987; revised edition 1996.

FEB *Finite and Eternal Being.* Translation of *Endliches und Ewiges Sein.* Translated by Kurt Reinhardt. Collected Works of Edith Stein 9. Washington, D.C.: ICS Publications, forthcoming. Page references from 3d German edition of 1986.

GL *Ganzheitliches Leben: Schriften zur religiösen Bildung.* Edith Steins Werke 12. Freiburg: Herder, 1990. ICS Publications translation forthcoming. Page references from German edition of 1990.

HL *The Hidden Life: Essays, Meditations, Spiritual Texts.* Translation of *Verborgenes Leben.* Translated by Waltraut Stein. Collected Works of Edith Stein 4. Washington, D.C.: ICS Publications, 1992.

KF *Knowledge and Faith.* Translation of *Erkenntnis und Glaube.* Translated by Walter Redmond. Collected Works of Edith Stein 8. Washington, D.C.: ICS Publications, 2000.

LJF *Life in a Jewish Family.* Translation of *Aus dem Leben einer jüdischen Familie.* Translated by Josephine Koeppel. Collected Works of Edith Stein 1. Washington, D.C.: ICS Publications, 1986.

MC *The Mystery of Christmas.* Translation of *Das Weihnachtsmysterium.* Translated by Josephine Rucker. Darlington, England: Carmelite Press, 1985.

PE *On the Problem of Empathy.* Translation of *Zum Problem der Einfühlung.* Translated by Waltraut Stein. 2d edition. The Hague: Martinus Nijhoff, 1970. 3d revised edition: Collected Works of Edith Stein 3. Washington, D.C.: ICS Publications, 1989.

PPH *Philosophy of Psychology and the Humanities.* Translation of *Beiträge zur philosophischen Begründung der Psychologie und der Geisteswissenschaften.* Translated by Mary Catherine Baseheart and Marianne Sawicki. Collected Works of Edith Stein 7. Washington, D.C.: ICS Publications, 2000.

SC *The Science of the Cross.* Translation of *Kreuzeswissenschaft.* Translated by Josephine Koeppel. Collected Works of Edith Stein 6. Washington, D.C.: ICS Publications, forthcoming. Page references from German edition of 1950.

SPL *Self-Portrait in Letters.* Translation of *Selbstbildnis in Briefen.* Translated by Josephine Koeppel. Collected Works of Edith Stein 5. Washington, D.C.: ICS Publications, 1993.

Introduction

Resilient in Hope

Edith Stein (1891–1942), like any canonized saint, is first and foremost a gift of God for the church. "In crowning their merits, you crown your own gifts," is the praise the Preface for the Saints in the *Sacramentary* directs to God. They are a "gift" because they have allowed the gifts of God visible in them to predominate throughout their lives.

St. Paul reminds us that there are "many different gifts" (1 Cor. 12:4; Rom. 12:6) among the faithful and the saints. Edith Stein, in this vein, was a multifaceted person of diverse gifts. The church's process of discernment concluded she was someone who more than adequately qualified for sainthood; it acknowledged proof both of the heroic virtues in her life and of a death that fit the Vatican's definition of martyrdom. In usual practice just one or the other is sufficient grounds to open the door to beatification for a "Servant of God." In the case of Edith Stein the church wished to stress that it was her witness both in life and in death that merited this recognition.

As a leading thinker in the Catholic women's movements of the German-speaking countries, a scholar of depth and originality, a proficient and prolific writer, and finally one of the millions of Jewish descent wiped out by the Nazis, she is a fitting representative of what Vatican Council II termed the "joys and hopes, the griefs and anguish" of the twentieth century.

Though born before that century began, her life's arc shows features close in rhythm and tone to our own. Her lessons continue. Much of what she did and wrote provides good advice for us to come to grips with the world around us, to contribute to it, and thus to prepare a richer future. Before considering that advice, it is worthwhile to review the life in which it was rooted.

When Edith Stein was canonized in 1998 she was the first Jewish-born Christian since the days of the early church to be added to the roster of the saints. She was the last of seven surviving children born to a Jewish couple in what was then still the German city of Breslau (now Wroclaw in Poland). Before she was two her fifty-year-old father died of sunstroke. Although she was raised in an observant home, by the time she was a teenager she had ceased to practice her Jewish faith and considered herself an atheist. Later, in spite of abundant intellectual gifts that opened the way to university studies, she slipped into a depressed state and found herself "wishing to be run over by some vehicle" in the street.

During World War I she earned a doctoral degree in philosophy with full honors under the direction of her admired mentor Edmund Husserl, founder of the school of phenomenology. Significantly, she wrote her dissertation on the theme of "empathy." She was one of the first women in Germany to earn a doctorate, and her brilliance was such that Husserl asked her to serve as his assistant, a position she filled for a year and a half. Nevertheless, the prevalent gender discrimination of the times prevented her from finding a university appointment. Instead, she became a faculty member at a teachers' training college for young women in the historic town of Speyer. When she did later receive a position at the Catholic pedagogical institute in Münster, she was soon dismissed as a result of the anti-Semitic legislation imposed by the new Nazi regime.

Throughout this period, Stein's spiritual life was marked by an earnest quest. Gradually she found herself questioning and ultimately abandoning her atheistic outlook, until eventually she decided to receive baptism as a Catholic in January of 1922. The next decade of her life was devoted to growing assimilation of all that her new-found faith offered and also to assisting Catholic women in their growth professionally and at home. At Speyer she taught equally by word and by lifestyle, since she led an exemplary life as a laywoman.

The sadness that her Jewish mother, Auguste Stein, experienced at Edith's baptism affected Edith deeply, and she was forced to bear up under yet more maternal distress when she decided to enter a Discalced Carmelite monastery in 1933. As much as this choice left her mother despondent, the adoption of religious life was the fulfillment of a dream Edith had nourished from the time of her baptism. The advent of Germany's anti-Semitic laws, which made it impossible for her to teach, offered a further inducement to take this step.

The years in Carmel brought her new responsibilities; still, her superiors invited her to write articles, then books, to share her talents with a wider audience. Her mother died at home in Breslau while Edith was a junior professed nun in Cologne Carmel. From there she saw members of her family start emigrating from an increasingly intolerant Germany, especially in the wake of the violence wreaked on the Jews by *Kristallnacht*, the infamous pogrom of November 9–10, 1938. Though now a nun in perpetual vows she too felt the pressure of Nazi anti-Semitism. For her own safety and that of her community she went into exile on the last day of that year. The Discalced Carmelite nuns in Holland welcomed her to their monastery in the little town of Echt.

But this move offered only temporary refuge. In 1940 Germany occupied Holland and Belgium and implemented their persecution of the Jews. Stein's status as a religious did not protect her. After the Catholic bishops of the country courageously took a stand against the Nazis' anti-Semitic measures, all the Catholic Jewish converts in Holland were deported to concentration camps.

On August 2, 1942, she and her sister Rosa, now too a convert to Catholicism, were seized during an SS raid. A few days later, in a transit concentration camp located in northern Holland, she told a visitor of her horror-filled apprehension for the well-being of her fellow deportees in these words: "I never knew people could actually be like this... and I honestly had no idea of how my brothers and sisters were being made to suffer." She took special measures in the days ahead to care for the terrified and neglected children in the camp. She provided for them a share in the support she had once described in one of her philosophical treatises: "In the knowledge that being holds me, I rest securely. This security, however, is not the self-assurance of one who under her own power stands on firm ground, but rather the sweet and blissful security of the child that is lifted up and carried by a strong arm" (see "Letting God's Plan Guide Us").

Radiating her inner strength and peace of spirit to all in the concentration camps Edith Stein went to her death on August 9, 1942, one week after her arrest, in a gas chamber at the Auschwitz/Birkenau death camp. Forty-five years later Pope John Paul II declared her Blessed in Cologne on May 1, 1987, and then proceeded to canonize her in 1998. Less than a year later he proclaimed her co-patroness of Europe along with St. Bridget of Sweden and St. Catherine of Siena.

The wisdom of Edith Stein was not simply the fruit of intellectual genius. In the crucible of human suffering she learned what *sym*pathy, or suffering *with* others, could do to alleviate their burdens. In the midst of her sometimes jumbled existence she provided an unintended epitaph in a sentence formulated in her magnum opus, *Finite and Eternal Being:* "What was not included in my plan lay in God's plan." Regardless of what happened to her, she embraced God's plan with hope, confident that "from God's point of view nothing is accidental," trusting it would lead her through all the trying situations life sent her way. That spirit of trust in divine providence is one of the key legacies of her life.

Committed Spirituality

The stress of contemporary living frequently induces an impulse to withdraw inward. People care intensively for their own small group, while regarding others with fearful suspicion. This attitude often overflows into their religious loyalty, causing them to be satisfied with mere rote repetition of standard tenets. Edith Stein never gave into such parochialism. She embodied a spirituality that was always open and connected to her surroundings.

At the time of Stein's canonization an introduction to her philosophical thought was published with the significant title *Person in the World*. Those four words capture a deep truth about her. Edith Stein always strove to craft accurate descriptions of the nature of the human person, and she always considered the person in direct relation to the world, our home — a temporary home perhaps (Heb. 13:14), but our current home nonetheless. One could not be abstracted from the other; both the human person and the world go together in Stein's thought and spirituality.

Maintaining her coherence of thought, Stein kept a vigilant eye to hold those two realities together and to avoid artificial opposition. Among her spiritual attitudes this was a guiding principle: never to lose contact with the real world, never to underestimate the salvific plan of God for creation (see Gen. 1:31). Despite its fallen condition, the world remains the theater where the drama of God's designs for our happiness and sanctification takes place. For this reason she applied her gifts of sharp observation to discern the "signs of the times," to keep in touch with the ups and downs, the ins and outs of salvation history and its current throughout her life. Many a disappointment and contretemps encountered along the way offered her ample reason to check out or close in on herself: when employment was denied her on account of her sex, or later on account of her Jewish birth. And yet she went on seeking to observe and plumb the hidden meaning of it all.

The motivational force that led her to remain open is described in a letter she wrote while still a laywoman to her friend Sister Callista Kopf on February 12, 1928: "I realized that something else is asked of us in this world and that, even in the contemplative life, one may not sever the connection with the world. I even believe that the deeper one is drawn into God, the more one must 'go out of oneself'; that is, one must go to the world in order to carry the divine life into it."

At the time of this writing it was just a little over six years since her baptism, which had followed by only a few months a fateful evening when she had stayed up all night reading the *Autobiography* of St. Teresa of Avila, concluding, by morning, with the exclamation "This is the truth." The great St. Teresa had opened the door to her; she developed a resultant desire to seek out a contemplative life like Teresa's. An experienced spiritual director, however, had convinced her to defer such an ambition for the time being and in the meantime to place her great intellectual gifts in the service of other Catholic women. Thus, in her letter to Sister Callista she assured her friend that "in this world" we shouldn't break our links to the world even if "thoughts of the Divine . . . in the contemplative life" are so admirable and desirable. On the contrary, closer proximity to God or "the deeper one is drawn into God" invariably leads a person "out of oneself" and "to the world in order to carry the divine life into it." We do not turn away from the world, we do not shun it, nor do we act as if it does not exist. Rather, we draw upon our relationship with God to "carry" or spread its fruits wherever they will do the most good.

The deep import of this passage is the expression she put within quotation marks: "go out of oneself." With it she evoked the Greek term *exstasis,* drawing on Pseudo-Dionysius. However, she chose to broaden the notion of "ecstasy," which is usually taken in an introverted and mystical way, and thus passed beyond the realm of visionary delights to establish the idea of an ecstatic act of *sharing*. We must not stay transfixed solely where and when we feel most uplifted in our enjoyment of an altered-state experience; rather, we should allow ourselves to go out to others, reassuring them on the basis of our experience that God does indeed lift us up. God is present and concerned with us. We establish contact with others in this kind of ecstasy because God wishes us to do so. We are sent from contact with the Divinity to proclaim that the "divine life" can be reached by all. A little further on in her letter, Stein expands on this, advising that one should "consider oneself totally as an instrument, especially with regard to the abilities one uses.... We are to see them as something used, not by us, but by God in us."

At a time when "flight from the world," or *fuga mundi,* was the safe recipe for any Catholic earnestly searching to lead a holy life, Stein said one can find God *in* the world by bringing God to the world. Adapt your abilities to the people and the situation, and God will take over as God wields the instrument his grace has finely tuned. Stein's corrective to what had become a classic principle of religious life slipped deftly between the opposed dangers of mere passivity on the one hand and spiritual hubris on the other. This is practical advice since it avoids the expected (for those times) exhortation to heavenly considerations of an altogether ethereal sort. "Something else is asked of us in this world," she wrote, so leave enjoyment of spiritual delights to the next world's state of rest. The proper forum for spiritual exchange between humans and God is right here. We court a great risk by thinking we can find it in a refined atmosphere devoid of real-life situations.

In canonizing Edith Stein the church points in the direction of a spirituality that includes new forms, "beginning with people as they are... in ways they can understand." To ask them to abandon their nature and aspire to a higher realm runs the risk of creating a dichotomy between the spiritual and the ordinary. Edith Stein says balance is attainable, and she would hardly have recommended it unless she thought it possible.

Compassion for Hesitant Pilgrims

The tendency of people to focus on their own clan or societal group leads them to disregard the sufferings and needs of others. They cannot be bothered by the "troubles" of others because they feel overburdened by their own. Edith Stein followed another way, the way of compassion for her worried and harried fellow travelers; and she offered a model for exercising compassion toward others.

As a laywoman, Edith Stein was well attuned to the preoccupations of her students. Many hours of counseling troubled individuals led her to write the following lines that show her keen empathy as a teacher: "Surely the children who attend convent schools should gain there the strength to form their lives in the spirit of Christ. Surely it is most important that the teachers truly have this spirit themselves and vividly exemplify it. . . . Today's young generation has passed through so many crises — it can no longer understand us, but we must make the effort to understand them; then perhaps we may yet be able to be of some help to them."

Stein wrote these words in October of 1932. For the young German women of whom she speaks it was one of those "between-the-wars" years when Germany lurched back and forth in societal and political upheaval that only increased with the Nazis' rise to power. W. H. Auden described the century accurately as an "Age of Anxiety." Edith was taking the proper measure of the raw material fed into her classroom when she claimed on behalf of her students the presence of "so many crises." Every generation has shifting matrices for its growth pains; only the perceptive educators like Edith Stein have both the insight and the courage to declare candidly what they are. And yet, beyond the shifts, Edith's words designate also what can be termed a "generation gap," and they call for compassion toward the alienation of youth that requires extra efforts to ease communication and to take the initiative.

Stein's great concern about the troubles of the people she taught carried through to care for children in the very final stage of her life. Arrested on August 2, 1942, by the SS, she died one week later not very far from her home city of Breslau in the Auschwitz extermination camp. In that last week of her life she passed through the infernal network of Hitler's "final solution." She saw two intermediate transit camps in Holland, first Amersfoort, and then Westerbork. Others who passed through Westerbork have described the deep sense of despair that overcame women with children in the camp. Understandably, the children were neglected, and an eyewitness account shows that Edith Stein did much to look after them. As Julius Marcan, a survivor, testified, "It was Edith Stein's complete calm and self-possession that marked her out from the rest of the prisoners. . . . Many of the mothers were on the brink of insanity and had sat moaning for days, without giving any thought to their children. Edith Stein immediately set about taking care of these little ones. She washed them, combed their hair, and tried to make sure they were fed and cared for."

From Westerbork Edith was able to send back a compelling message to the nuns at her monastery in Echt: "We place our trust in your prayers. There are so many persons here in need of a little comfort, and they expect it from the sisters." She had only herself to give: her attentiveness, the time she took away from her own worries, and her sense of religious hope. She gave all that she had, because she was fully present with and to the others, and she was willing to do as much as she could to share their burden of suffering so as to lighten the load. She acted as a compassionate sister to the suffering, to "be of some help to them."

Loving Knowledge of the Faith

It is commonly observed among seminarians or younger religious today that, while they abound in zeal to serve the church and extend its outreach, they often lack a grasp of fundamentals of their faith. Edith Stein would have regarded this as a deficiency, and in her own way she worked to rectify it.

Her last major writing project was a commentary on St. John of the Cross, noted mystic and collaborator of St. Teresa of Avila in the reform of Carmel. He was declared a Doctor of the Church in 1926, and her book, *Science of the Cross,* was to be a contribution to the fourth centenary celebrations of his birth in 1942. Due to her arrest by the SS the manuscript lacks some finishing touches and a formal conclusion. She made the following trenchant remark in the introduction, entitled "Meaning and Basis of the Science of the Cross": "Many Christians feel depressed because the events of the Gospel do not — or do no longer — impress them as they ought and fail to affect and shape their lives. The example of the saints shows how it ought to be: where there is truly living faith there Christian doctrine and the mighty deeds of God are the content of life which shape everything and before which everything else must give way. . . . If a saintly soul thus assimilates the truths of faith they become the science of the saints. If the mystery of the cross becomes its inner form it grows into the science of the cross."

This perceptive and timely passage houses an acute preoccupation of St. Edith. After judging the generalized world situation with deserved reservation, she moved on to the religious sphere as part of a general malaise. Christians were depressed because they, like others, did not "react to facts according to their true value." Unfortunately, they shared in a "lack of sensibility" to reality because they showed less than a "truly living faith." Her estimate of the situation did not flow from pessimism, but from realism. Sr. Teresa Benedicta wrote her study on St. John of the Cross during World War II, and the judgment of history confirms her sense of a real paralysis and breakdown in morale that allowed so many atrocities to occur.

Stein assigned a cause for the state of depression among Christians. She claimed that if "Christian doctrine and the mighty deeds of God . . . [were] the content of [their] life" they would react to events differently. What is lacking is effective assimilation of the faith on the part of those who by the rebirth of baptism are expected to participate actively in the church. In fact, Stein used the word "assimilate" twice, and made it the heart of the matter. If alive today she would call upon the church to supply more effective ways to assimilate the riches of the faith. Ever an alert pedagogue, now a canonized saint, she continues to stand for an intellectual apostolate among Catholics. She also reminds us that effective catechetical methods and outreach are indispensable means to meaningful participation by Catholics in all dimensions of public life, be they directly related to the church or found in the mainstream of secular life.

If believers die of hunger for want of proper understanding of the teachings transmitted to them from Christ in the Good News of Salvation, the world will lack the beneficial leaven that Christianity can offer. In parallel fashion, Stein's text warns about a diminishment of holiness in our midst: there will be no science of the cross at work because those who are called to be saints will hardly craft it into that "inner form" they would educe out of the "truths of the faith." The blockage they suffer and the lost contact with Gospel values will stunt their growth. Edith Stein invested in a deepening process of her faith; from her baptism onward she considered assimilation of the faith an extremely precious exercise of her life. Not even monastic life kept her from culling from her own ongoing experience lessons capable of sharing growth in the knowledge of the faith. During the first few years in the monastery at Cologne she wrote concise articles about spiritually significant persons or themes from Carmelite history and placed them in various German newspapers. What she did showed she would not just lament poor knowledge of the faith in others; instead she strove to make up for the deficiencies. Healthy vigilance of that kind will remedy flagging knowledge and promote better appreciation of the faith in the future.

Respect for Riches of the Spirit in Those Seeking God with "Sincere Hearts"

Edith Stein highly prized her relationship to the Jewish people and their religion. There was no root incompatibility for her between being a Christian and her esteem for Judaism. She supposedly told her pious mother that as a Catholic she had come to appreciate as never before the grace-bearing elements that Judaism offered. It was, ironically, the discovery of Christ and his cross that had for her opened her eyes to those wellsprings of grace. Stein's appreciation and gratitude for her Jewish roots are reflected in the fact that she chose to write a loving memoir of her childhood, *Life in a Jewish Family,* at precisely the time when anti-Semitic hatred was breaking out in Germany.

The way Edith related to her mother is paradigmatic for the way she related to her former religion. Her mother was for her an alter ego in so many ways, not only as she was growing up but in all the phases of her life. Tenacity, honesty, and devotion were three precious values Edith derived from Auguste Stein. Her attitude toward her mother's death clarifies extremely well Stein's respect for the way God works in other religions. Regard for the signs of God's presence beyond the borders of her own faith system was carefully maintained and recommended by Edith Stein.

Auguste Stein died on September 14, 1936. Edith included news of her mother's passing in nine letters in all. Every one of them shows Edith admiring the faith of Auguste and the fruits of her God-fearing life. Perhaps the most significant of them was sent on October 4, 1936, to Sr. Callista Kopf, the same recipient of her letter from 1928 about ecstasy. With the following words it stated the reason why Stein felt her mother had gone to heaven, even as it excluded any possibility her mother might have converted to Christianity: "The news of her conversion was a totally unfounded rumor. I have no idea who made it up. My mother held to her faith to the very last. The faith and firm confidence she had in her God from her earliest childhood to her eighty-seventh year remained steadfast, and were the last things that stayed alive in her during the final difficult agony. Therefore, I have the firm belief that she found a very merciful judge and is now my most faithful helper on my way, so that I, too, may reach my goal."

By being always faithful and true to her belief in her own God Frau Stein found a "very merciful" judge at the end of her days. Fidelity to the faith of her ancestors saw her through and crowned her perseverance, even in spite of the final "agony" caused by a stomach tumor. In referring to the trust her mother had in the Lord Edith notes it was the "firm confidence she had in *her* God." The basis of her religious respect is not so much the presence of any good deeds her mother did, but that "firm confidence" that fed her mother's devotion for the God of Israel. In spite of the difference between her and her mother, Edith esteemed her tenacious devotion, nor would she think to criticize it in the least.

The epistolary remarks taken together prove Edith adopted an enlightened stance toward interreligious relations between Catholics and Jews. Oftentimes harsh and hurt feelings arise around her status as a convert, but greater awareness of the "spiritual ecumenism" she cultivated would defuse a good number of the emotional reactions her name can provoke. Further confirmation comes from what she wrote about the second most influential adult in her life, her revered "Master" Edmund Husserl. As the Protestant founder of phenomenology lay dying, she penned a letter to her sister phenomenologist Adelgundis Jaegerschmid, which contained these far-seeing thoughts: "I am not at all worried about my dear Master. It has always been far from me to think that God's mercy allows itself to be circumscribed by the visible church's boundaries. God is truth. All who seek truth seek God, whether this is clear to them or not."

Integrated "Vita Devota"

The Catholic Church today often reflects a certain stress between groups that take divergent stances regarding the content and rate of renewal since the Second Vatican Council. Even though Vatican II remains the reference point and rich watershed of efforts toward revitalized church life, there is a desire on the part of some to return to practices that held sway before that great ecclesial event. Longing for a "golden age" of liturgical practice (something that never actually existed anyway, though they don't usually grant that point), they want no more changes in liturgical observance and even flirt with temptations to reinstall abandoned rituals. In this area of mystagogy and liturgical piety one finds a path forward with the help of Edith Stein.

The year 1937 marked a midpoint in Edith's growth in her vocation as a Catholic contemplative nun. She had entered Carmel late in 1933 and would die in the summer of 1942 at Auschwitz. She had ample opportunity to delve into Carmelite spirituality and form herself in the mold of monastic life. This did not mean, as some feared, she was losing contact with usual church life around her. On the contrary, she kept keenly in tune with the ebb and flow of events and even the surges of disagreement that can occur.

One such disagreement concerned the liturgy, the "prayer of the church" that she had found so nourishing and important for her spiritual life. The situation can be summed up as follows: a clash over the proper balance between liturgical and individual piety was brewing from the midthirties on, primarily in Germany. Some felt that renewed liturgical practices would offer an adequate source of inspiration and make it possible to do away with devotional practices of more recent vintage. Those who favored the latter opposed the liturgical partisans and branded liturgical practices as "externalist" and "activist" with harmful consequences for individual spiritual progress. A solution suggesting coexistence between the two concerns, i.e., between ritual participation and interiority, would be the obvious answer, but when controversies move toward a flash point they tend to invite extreme formulations that often further widen the breach.

Sr. Teresa Benedicta of the Cross knew well the mentality of the liturgists: she had had frequent contacts with the archabbot of Beuron, the famous South German Benedictine abbey, and had worshiped there during school vacation time. On the other hand, but not in opposition to the Benedictine vision of worship in common, she also had opted to join the Carmelites, an order known for its promotion of silent, meditative prayer with a mostly austere devotional style.

She decided to offer ideas from her own experience to ease the rising tension at that time. The result was a small essay/treatise called *The Prayer of the Church,* published in 1937 in a book that offered other essays weighing some of the factors involved in the ongoing debate in Germany. Her reflection was a clear attempt to strike a balance, and the following passage (taken from the full text of the essay found in the selection "Daily Work, 'A Single Liturgy' ") demonstrates how successful she was in doing so: "The monks 'resembling angels' surround the altar of sacrifice and make sure that the praise of God does not cease, as in heaven so on earth. The solemn prayers they recite as the resonant mouth of the church frame the holy sacrifice. They also frame, permeate, and consecrate all other 'daily work' so that prayer and work become a single *opus Dei,* a single 'liturgy.' "

As in so many other passages of Stein's works the very terminology she adopts houses clues to understanding. Three points emerge from her creative insight. She stressed the two major axes of public worship, namely, the Eucharist and the Liturgy of the Hours. They are described in nonpragmatic terms, too, so Stein avoids what is sometimes called the "service station" model of liturgy, or one that subordinates worship to the moral effects it produces after worship time is over. The words "*praise* of God" and "resonant *mouth* of the church" bear this out. The monks are granted by vocation a holy leisure (*otium sacrum*) that allows more time; thus it is easier for them to embellish praise by the beautiful cadences of their singing. Still, all liturgy, wherever it is celebrated, needs to stress gratuitous praise of God, and Stein reminds us of this. Her text goes further.

She then links the prayers of the monks to activities outside the worship area, because those prayers are also a setting for (they "frame") daily work, and they both permeate and consecrate that work. Our faith vision posits a difference between cultic and noncultic activities but not a gap between them. Benedictines themselves take for inspiration the motto "Ora *et* labora." The same can be said for differences between cultic acts and acts of piety by individuals or smaller prayer groups: they might take place according to different rhythms, but they do not call for a choice of one over the other, certainly not one against the other.

Finally, Stein claims there is a unified notion embracing both worship and noncultic acts: prayer and work, she wrote, "become a single *opus Dei,* a single 'liturgy.' " When one bases individual prayer on the Mass and the prayer of the Hours, when one infuses daily work with them both, work acquires a spirit of service of God (*opus Dei*). To the extent work is directed to praising God in the Mass and in the Hours it becomes "liturgy," whose root meaning is "work of the people." It seems Stein was trying to bridge the gap between worship and work in themselves, as much as she wanted to close the widening gap between the liturgical enthusiasts and the pietists. Her insight can help worship flow over smoothly into daily tasks; and the fulfillment of those tasks can itself prove to be worshipful activity. This requires vigilance in a hyper-busy world, so full of excuses to avoid forms of godly activity, but Stein reassures us that the challenge is worth accepting. No genuine Christian spirituality can survive without the integration of both liturgy and devotion that she promoted.

The "emphases" above accompanied other spiritual interests of Edith Stein/Sr. Teresa Benedicta. They obviously do not overshadow attention paid by her to such questions as the relations between men and women, contacts between philosophy and the theological enterprise, empathy and faith, or religious experience. One could add still others such as the education of children, individual and communal rights and obligations, peace and violence, co-responsible living in society, especially in the face of a quickly expanding consumerism, or the role of the church in the protection of the persecuted.

Attention to Edith Stein is on the rise since her canonization. Sensitive individuals will mine her thought for new lessons of hope for new generations. She would be busy doing that very thing if she were still alive. And her courage to come to grips with reality as an ever-alert person, seeking the truth, will surely attract others to follow in her footsteps.

1

In and For the Life of the World

✝

At the time Edith Stein requested baptism the Catholic Church in her part of Europe was undergoing a period of creative ferment. Throughout the 1920s and 1930s she was in touch with many of the leading Catholic thinkers of the day, including Dietrich Von Hildebrand (philosopher), Raphael Walzer (liturgy), Peter Wust (philosopher), Max Scheler (philosopher), Gertrud von le Fort (author), Johannes Quasten (patrologist), Erich Przywara (spiritual writer), and the French philosopher Jacques Maritain (whom she met near Paris). They were more than just names out of books; they were esteemed colleagues who shared her dream to enhance the contemporary relevance of the church and to increase its effectiveness in fulfilling its mission in the world. Romano Guardini referred to this period as an attempt to recapture the "springtime of the church," a time for fresh contacts with the world in which they lived.

Edith took up the challenge to build bridges between trends of Catholic thought and cultural forms outside the church's boundaries. She believed, with the others, that the Catholic Church's relations with society had grown brittle and that new efforts were required to interact more directly with reality and to serve the world as a creative leaven. In this task she relied on at least two sources for guidance. First, her training as a phenomenologist told her to let things speak for themselves, to allow the "thing itself" to shine forth in its own identity. She had to look long and carefully at the many facets of reality, permitting them to speak to her before deriving analyses of what she observed. She showed respect for things, the better to stay in dialogue with them. Second, she drew on the experience of St. Teresa of Avila, a saint who always wed mysticism to a burning zeal for renewal in her own time. Teresa called prayer a "way of perfection," not a way toward introspective perfectionism. Prayer for her went hand-in-hand with alertness to the needs of the church in her time. Edith Stein appreciated the fact that Teresa lived in tiempos recios, *or troubled times at the end of the medieval era, and yet* la Madre *was able to hit on a format for her burning devotion that enabled her to contribute to the betterment of the world she knew. Edith would not avoid contact with an ailing world, but she determined to help remedy its illnesses by the constructive activities of teaching, lecturing, writing, and then finally embracing the very lifestyle — of a Discalced Carmelite nun — that Teresa had transmitted as a living heritage to the church.*

She summed up her conviction that a committed, connected stance is the only one possible for modern Christians in class notes prepared for delivery in the 1932 summer semester in Münster: "The church as the kingdom of God in this world should reflect changes in human thought. Only by accepting each age as it is and treating it according to its singular nature can the church bring eternal truth and life to temporality."

HER SPECIAL KIND OF ECSTASY

Stein believed that intense contact with God, far from being an escape from reality, leads one inescapably to share God's concern for all created things. Flowing from such loving contact with the Creator comes a willingness to extend oneself to others in acts of generous interchange. Stein learned this lesson over time, as she explains in this letter to a religious friend.

St. Magdalena, Speyer, February 12, 1928

Dear Sister Callista,

I would have liked to answer the kind greetings you sent for the Feast of the Purification [the anniversary of Edith's Confirmation] much sooner, but it was impossible. And since I know I shall soon be interrupted, I will get at once to the heart of your letter and answer your principal question.

Of course, religion is not something to be relegated to a quiet corner or for a few festive hours, but rather, as you yourself perceive, it must be the root and basis of all life: and, not merely for a few chosen ones, but for every true Christian (though of these there is still but a "little flock"). That it is possible to worship God by doing scholarly research is something I learned, actually, only when I was busy with [the translation of] St. Thomas [Aquinas's *Quaestiones de Veritate* from Latin into German]. (In the little booklet that the Sisters here use for the Thomas Sundays, there is a beautiful meditation about that.) Only thereafter could I decide to resume serious scholarly research.

Immediately before, and for a good while after my conversion, I was of the opinion that to lead a religious life meant one had to give up all that was secular and to live totally immersed in thoughts of the Divine. But gradually I realized that something else is asked of us in this world and that, even in the contemplative life, one may not sever the connection with the world. I even believe that the deeper one is drawn into God, the more one must "go out of oneself" [allusion to "ecstasy" treated by Pseudo-Dionysius in his work *The Divine Names*]; that is, one must go to the world in order to carry the divine life into it.

The only essential is that one finds, first of all, a quiet corner in which one can communicate with God as though there were nothing else, and that must be done daily. It seems to me the best time is in the early morning hours before we begin our daily work; furthermore, it is also essential that one accepts one's particular mission there, preferably for each day, and does not make one's own choice. Finally, one is to consider oneself totally an instrument, especially with regard to the abilities one uses to perform one's special tasks, in our case, e.g., intellectual ones. We are to see them as something used, not by us, but by God in us.

This, then, is my recipe, and I presume that Sr. Dolorosa's will not be very different; so far I have never talked to her about it. My life begins anew each morning, and ends every evening; I have neither plans nor prospects beyond it: i.e., to plan ahead could obviously be part of one's daily duties — teaching school, for example, could be impossible without that — but it must never turn into a "worry" about the coming day.

After all that, you will understand why I cannot agree when you say I have "become" someone. It does appear as though the orbit of my daily duties is to expand. But that, in my opinion, does not change anything about me. It has been demanded of me, and I have undertaken it, although I am still in the dark about what it will comprise, and what the routine will consist of. I shall be thinking of you on the 15th.

I would appreciate your allowing Sr. Agnella [Stadtmüller] to read this letter, for I cannot write another one to her now. But do so only if you like the idea. Otherwise just give both of the Sisters my warmest regards and au revoir. After all, they will be coming here soon.

Most cordially, your
Edith Stein

—SPL, 54–55

A DIFFERENT ECSTASY AGAIN

The Thomist *was the first American journal to publish one of Stein's writings in English. Her text was titled "Ways to Know God." It was an essay on the "symbolic theology" of Pseudo-Dionysius, the Neoplatonist Christian mystical writer of the fifth–sixth century. As she examined the theme of beauty in its relation to God and the world she returned — thirteen years after her letter to Sr. Callista Kopf — to the notion of other-centered ecstasy. Love, for her, is "ecstatic."*

When we consider the names that Holy Scripture has coined for God, we find that almost all are founded upon the effects of his divine goodness. He is called *one* in virtue of the unity by which we are one and are led to a godlike unity. He is *wise* and *beautiful,* because all things, if they keep their nature intact, are full of divine harmony and holy beauty, etc.

Thus it is proper for him who is the Cause of all things and is above all things to have no names, yet at the same time to have all names of all things. He is fittingly named after all things, since he has anticipated everything in a simple, unbounded manner through the perfect goodness in his providence that brings everything about. While being and remaining *one* — in a sense of "oneness" going beyond anything we have access to — he nonetheless sets forth a multiplicity from himself and this is why he can be grasped.

God's "procession" should be taken in several ways. In his second chapter Dionysius treats processions in the exclusive sense, those within the Godhead through which the *one* divine being unfolds in three persons. The divine names here treated are based on the outward procession of the Godhead as a whole in the works of creation.

Dionysius recognizes a twofold multiplicity mediating between the one God and the diversity of the sense world: the world of created pure spirits — the "celestial hierarchy" — and the world of pure "ideas" or "essences," from which the names of God are taken. It was mentioned in the beginning that the heavenly spirits, too, play a key role in our knowledge of God. But this is not the question here; it rather concerns that impersonal, intermediate realm. They are treated in this work only insofar as they, the highest of all creatures, along with everything created, have the origin of their being in the first One, the "Primal Be-ing," "Over-Be-ing." Dionysius does not appeal to Plato, but it is precisely in this work that the Platonist is unmistakable.

The first divine name he considers — the one most properly applying to the divine essence — is *"good."* As *goodness* itself, the good in itself, good by its very being, it radiates goodness to all be-ings, as the sun illuminates everything receptive in some way to its light, by merely being, not in virtue of some thought or intent. (The sun, however, is to the good only as a poor copy is to the original.) To the good every be-ing — from the highest spirits to be-ings lacking reason and life — owes its being and all that it is, its ranking and conformity to law, its share in the good and its tending toward the good. For as in the visible realm everything makes for the light, so every be-ing strives after the good, each in its very own way. But to the highest spirits it is especially proper to radiate back the divine good and turn toward the good what is subordinate to it. Thus the good, as bound up with being, stands above all be-ing, and, as bound up with being, it is at the same time bound up with form whereby the formless is formed.

The platonic purport is perhaps more clearly in evidence in Dionysius's explanation of the *beautiful.* The good as such is also called "the beautiful" or "beauty." The two — the beautiful and beauty — should not be separated in the oneness of the all-embracing Cause, while in be-ings what shares in beauty is called "beautiful" and what all things beautiful share in is called "beauty."

Supraessential beauty is called *beauty* as that which bestows an appropriate beauty on all things, elicits all harmony and all splendor in them, and calls and turns everything to itself as to the light.

But it is called *beautiful* as the wholly beautiful, over-beautiful, as what is beautiful ever and in the same way, neither coming to be nor passing away, neither increasing nor decreasing, not partly beautiful and partly ugly or for many beautiful but at times unbeautiful, not beautiful with respect to this and ugly with respect to that, not beautiful here but not there; not beautiful for some but not for others. It is rather so called as that which is always uniformly beautiful in itself and in harmony with itself, as that which possesses in itself, over-abundantly and beforehand, the original beauty of all that is beautiful.

For all beauty and all that is beautiful subsists beforehand simply in the simple and supernatural nature of everything beautiful. All things are beautiful in virtue of this, the beautiful, for it is the ground of the being of all things. All harmony and all commonness of be-ings subsists through it, for it guides everything to itself through love and unifies everything in this striving. It sets everything in motion and is the goal for whose sake everything comes to be. Just for this reason the beautiful and the good are the same: what everything strives for and what everything shares in.

Now, that which suffers not the Good to abide in itself but stirs it in an excess that brings forth all things and puts it to work is *Love*. For love is "ecstatic" [allusion to Pseudo-Dionysius's phrase "ecstatic power"] and makes the lover the possession of the beloved, as Paul says: "no longer I live but Christ lives in me."

And so we might even be so bold as to say that the Author of all things has been beside himself in the exuberance of his loving goodness: He goes out of himself without going out of himself and through his providence cares for every be-ing.

But he is called not only "Love," but "Beloved" as well. For in the creature he brings forth love for himself. As Love he bestirs himself, as the Beloved he bestirs creatures toward himself. Therein the divine love proves beginningless and endless, an everlasting cycle, wheeling, but for the sake of the good, from the good, in the good, toward the good. —KF, 132–34

WITHOUT BARRIERS IN THE WORLD

Edith Stein recognized the world as the theater of God's salvific activities because she felt we all belong to God and are interconnected. The only barriers we need fear are the ones we erect ourselves.

One with God. . . . If Christ is the Head and we the members in the Mystical Body, then we relate to each other as member to member and we are all one in God, a divine life. If God is in us and if he is love, then it cannot be otherwise but to love one another. Therefore, our love for our brothers and sisters is the measure of our love for God. But it is different from a natural, human love which affects this one or that who may be related to us, or who may be close to us because of the bonds of temperament or common interests. The rest are "strangers" who don't concern us, perhaps even by their presence annoy us, so that love is kept as far away as possible. For the Christian there is no "strange human being." He is in every instance the "neighbor" whom we have with us and who is most in need of us. It makes no difference whether he is related or not, whether we "like" him or not, whether he is "morally worthy" of help or not. The love of Christ knows no bounds, it never ceases, it never withdraws in the face of hatred or foul play. He came for the sake of sinners and not for the righteous. If the love of Christ lives in us, then we do as he did and seek after the lost sheep.

Natural love seeks to possess the beloved entirely and as

far as possible not to share him. Christ came to win back lost mankind for the Father: whoever loves with his love will want people for God and not for himself. Of course, that is the surest way to possess them forever; for wherever we have entrusted a person to God, then we are one with him in God, whereas the craving to overpower sooner or later always leads to loss. It is true of the other's soul as for one's own and for every external possession. Whoever is evidently out to win and to possess loses; whoever hands over to God, wins. —MC, 12–13

DAILY WORK, "A SINGLE LITURGY"

As a laywoman Edith Stein appreciated the gains of the liturgical movement in Germany. Then as a nun she joined a love for meditative prayer to her esteem for group worship. In her essay "The Prayer of the Church" she explained how to avoid any dichotomy between the two so prayer and life can always remain intertwined and mutually inspire each other.

"Through him, with him, and in him in the unity of the Holy Spirit, all honor and glory is yours, Almighty Father, for ever and ever." With these solemn words, the priest ends the eucharistic prayer at the center of which is the mysterious event of the consecration. These words at the same time encapsulate the prayer of the church: honor and glory to the triune God through, with, and in Christ. Although the words are directed to the Father, all glorification of the Father is at the same time glorification of the Son and of the Holy Spirit. Indeed, the prayer extols the majesty that the Father imparts to the Son and that both impart to the Holy Spirit from eternity to eternity.

All praise of God is through, with, and in Christ. Through him, because only through Christ does humanity have access to the Father and because his existence as God-man and his work of salvation are the fullest glorification of the Father; with him, because all authentic prayer is the fruit of union with Christ and at the same time buttresses this union, and because in honoring the Son one honors the Father and vice versa; in him, because the praying church is Christ himself, with every individual praying member as a part of his Mystical Body, and because the Father is in the Son and the Son the reflection of the Father, who makes his majesty visible. The dual meanings of through, with, and in clearly express the God-man's mediation.

The prayer of the church is the prayer of the ever-living Christ. Its prototype is Christ's prayer during his human life.

The Prayer of the Church as Liturgy and Eucharist

The Gospels tell us that Christ prayed the way a devout Jew faithful to the law prayed. Just as he made pilgrimages to Jerusalem at the prescribed times with his parents as a child, so he later journeyed to the temple there with his disciples to celebrate the high feasts. Surely he sang with holy enthusiasm along with his people the exultant hymns in which the pilgrim's joyous anticipation streamed forth: "I rejoiced when I heard them say: Let us go to God's house" (Ps. 122:1). From his last supper with his disciples, we know that Jesus said the old blessings over bread, wine, and the fruits of the earth, as they are prayed to this day. So he fulfilled one of the most sacred religious duties: the ceremonial Passover seder to commemorate deliverance from slavery in Egypt. And perhaps this very gathering gives us the profoundest glimpse into Christ's prayer and the key to understanding the prayer of the church.

> While they were at supper, he took bread, said the blessing, broke the bread, and gave it to his disciples, saying, "Take this, all of you, and eat it: this is my body which will be given up for you."
>
> In the same way, he took the cup, filled with wine. He gave you thanks, and giving the cup to his disciples, said,

> "Take this, all of you, and drink from it: this is the cup of my blood, the blood of the new and everlasting covenant. It will be shed for you and for all so that sins may be forgiven."

Blessing and distributing bread and wine were part of the Passover rite. But here both receive an entirely new meaning. This is where the life of the church begins. Only at Pentecost will it appear publicly as a Spirit-filled and visible community. But here at the Passover meal the seeds of the vineyard are planted that make the outpouring of the Spirit possible. In the mouth of Christ, the old blessings become life-giving words. The fruits of the earth become his body and blood, filled with his life. Visible creation, which he entered when he became a human being, is now united with him in a new, mysterious way. The things that serve to sustain human life are fundamentally transformed, and the people who partake of them in faith are transformed too, drawn into the unity of life with Christ and filled with his divine life. The Word's life-giving power is bound to the sacrifice. The Word became flesh in order to surrender the life he assumed, to offer himself and a creation redeemed by his sacrifice in praise to the Creator. Through the Lord's last supper, the Passover meal of the Old Covenant is converted into the Easter meal of the New Covenant: into the sacrifice on the cross at Golgotha and those joyous meals between Easter and Ascension when the disciples recognized the Lord in the breaking of bread, and into the sacrifice of the Mass with Holy Communion.

As the Lord took the cup, he gave thanks. This recalls the words of blessing thanking the Creator. But we also know that Christ used to give thanks when, prior to a miracle, he raised his eyes to his Father in heaven. He gives thanks because he knows in advance that he will be heard. He gives thanks for the divine power that he carries in himself and by means of which he will demonstrate the omnipotence of the Creator to human eyes.

He gives thanks for the work of salvation that he is permitted to accomplish, and through this work, which is in fact itself the glorification of the triune Godhead, because it restores this Godhead's distorted image to pure beauty. Therefore the whole perpetual sacrificial offering of Christ—at the cross, in the holy Mass, and in the eternal glory of heaven—can be conceived as a single great thanksgiving—as Eucharist: as gratitude for creation, salvation, and consummation. Christ presents himself in the name of all creation, whose prototype he is and to which he descended to renew it from the inside out and lead it to perfection. But he also calls upon the entire created world itself, united with him, to give the Creator the tribute of thanks that is his due. Some understanding of this eucharistic character of prayer had already been revealed under the Old Covenant. The wondrous form of the tent of meeting, and later, of Solomon's temple, erected as it was according to divine specifications, was considered an image of the entire creation, assembled in worship and service around its Lord. The tent around which the people of Israel camped during their wanderings in the wilderness was called the "home of God among us" (Exod. 38:21). It was thought of as a "home below" over against a "higher home." "O Lord, I love the house where you dwell, the place where your glory abides," sings the Psalmist (Ps. 26:8), because the tent of meeting is "valued as much as the creation of the world." As the heavens in the creation story were stretched out like a carpet, so carpets were prescribed as walls for the tent. As the waters of the earth were separated from the waters of the heavens, so the curtain separated the Holy of Holies from the outer rooms. The "bronze" sea is modeled after the sea that is contained by its shores. The seven-branched light in the tent stands for the heavenly lights. Lambs and birds stand for the swarms of life teeming in the water, on the earth, and in the air. And as the earth is handed over to people, so in the sanctuary there stands the high priest "who is purified to act and to serve before God." Moses blessed, anointed, and sanctified the completed house as the Lord blessed and sanctified the work of his hands on the seventh day. The Lord's house was to be a witness to God on earth just as heaven and earth are witnesses to him (Deut. 30:19).

In place of Solomon's temple, Christ has built a temple of living stones, the communion of saints. At its center, he stands as the eternal high priest; on its altar he is himself the perpetual sacrifice. And, in turn, the whole of creation is drawn into the "liturgy," the ceremonial worship service: the fruits of the earth as the mysterious offerings, the flowers and the lighted candlesticks, the carpets and the curtain, the ordained priest, and the anointing and blessing of God's house. Even the cherubim are not missing. Fashioned by the hand of the artist, the visible forms stand watch beside the Holy of Holies. And, as living copies of them, the "monks resembling angels" surround the sacrificial altar and make sure that the praise of God does not cease, as in heaven so on earth. The solemn prayers they recite as the resonant mouth of the church frame the holy sacrifice. They also frame, permeate, and consecrate all other "daily work," so that prayer and work become a single *opus Dei,* a single "liturgy." Their readings from the holy Scriptures and from the fathers, from the church's menologies and the teachings of its principal pastors, are a great, continually swelling hymn of praise to the rule of providence and to the progressive actualization of the eternal plan of salvation. Their morning hymns of praise call all of creation together to unite once more in praising the Lord: mountains and hills, streams and rivers, seas and lands and all that inhabit them, clouds and winds, rain and snow, all peoples of earth, every class and race of people, and finally also the inhabitants of heaven, the angels and the saints. Not only in representations giving them human form and made by human hands are they to participate in the great Eucharist of creation, but they are to be involved as personal beings — or better, we are to unite ourselves through our liturgy to their eternal praise of God.

"We" here refers not just to the religious who are called to give solemn praise to God, but to all Christian people. When these stream into cathedrals and chapels on holy days, when they joyously participate daily in worship using the "people's choral Mass" and the new "folk Mass" forms, they show that they are conscious of their calling to praise God. The liturgical unity of the heavenly with the earthly church, both of which thank God "through Christ," finds its most powerful expression in the preface and Sanctus of the Mass. However, the liturgy leaves no doubt that we are not yet full citizens of the heavenly Jerusalem, but pilgrims on the way to our eternal home. We must always prepare ourselves before we may dare to lift our eyes to the luminous heights and to unite our voices with the "holy, holy, holy" of the heavenly chorus. Each created thing to be used in the worship service must be withdrawn from its profane use, must be purified and consecrated. Before the priest climbs the steps to the altar, he must cleanse himself by acknowledging his sins, and the faithful must do so with him. Prior to each step as the offertory continues, he must repeat his plea for the forgiveness of sins — for himself and for those gathered around him as well as for all to whom the fruits of the sacrifice are to flow. The sacrifice itself is a sacrifice of expiation that transforms the faithful as it transforms the gifts, unlocks heaven for them, and enables them to sing a hymn of praise pleasing to God. All that we need to be received into the communion of saints is summed up in the seven petitions of the Our Father, which the Lord did not pray in his own name, but to instruct us. We say it before communion, and when we say it sincerely and from our hearts and receive communion in the proper spirit, it fulfills all of our petitions. Communion delivers us from evil, because it cleanses us of sin and gives us peace of heart that takes away the sting of all other "evils." It brings us the forgiveness of past sins and strengthens us in the face of temptations. It is itself the bread of life that we need daily to grow into eternal life. It makes our will into an instrument at

God's disposal. Thereby it lays the foundation for the kingdom of God in us and gives us clean lips and a pure heart to glorify God's holy name. So we see again how the offertory, communion, and the praise of God [in the Divine Office] are internally related. Participation in the sacrifice and in the sacrificial meal actually transforms the soul into a living stone in the city of God — in fact, each individual soul into a temple of God.

Solitary Dialogue with God as the Prayer of the Church

The individual human soul [as] a temple of God — this opens to us an entirely new, broad vista. The prayer life of Jesus was to be the key to understanding the prayer of the church. We saw that Christ took part in the public and prescribed worship services of his people, i.e., in what one usually calls "liturgy." He brought the liturgy into the most intimate relationship with his sacrificial offering and so for the first time gave it its full and true meaning — that of thankful homage of creation to its Creator. This is precisely how he transformed the liturgy of the Old Covenant into that of the New.

But Jesus did not merely participate in public and prescribed worship services. Perhaps even more often the Gospels tell of solitary prayer in the still of the night, on open mountain tops, in the wilderness far from people. Jesus' public ministry was preceded by forty days and forty nights of prayer. Before he chose and commissioned his twelve apostles, he withdrew into the isolation of the mountains. By his hour on the Mount of Olives, he prepared himself for his road to Golgotha. A few short words tell us what he implored of his Father during this most difficult hour of his life, words that are given to us as guiding stars for our own hours on the Mount of Olives. "Father, if you are willing, take this cup away from me. Nevertheless, let your will be done, not mine." Like lightning, these words for an instant illumine for us the innermost spiritual life of

Jesus, the unfathomable mystery of his God-man existence and his dialogue with the Father. Surely, this dialogue was life-long and uninterrupted. Christ prayed interiorly not only when he had withdrawn from the crowd, but also when he was among people. And once he allowed us to look extensively and deeply at this secret dialogue. It was not long before the hour of the Mount of Olives; in fact, it was immediately before they set out to go there at the end of the last supper, which we recognize as the actual hour of the birth of the church. "Having loved his own . . . , he loved them to the end." He knew that this was their last time together, and he wanted to give them as much as he in any way could. He had to restrain himself from saying more. But he surely knew that they could not bear any more, in fact, that they could not even grasp this little bit. The Spirit of Truth had to come first to open their eyes for it. And after he had said and done everything that he could say and do, he lifted his eyes to heaven and spoke to the Father in their presence. We call these words Jesus' great high priestly prayer, for this talking alone with God also had its antecedent in the Old Covenant. Once a year on the greatest and most holy day of the year, on the Day of Atonement, the high priest stepped into the Holy of Holies before the face of the Lord "to pray for himself and his household and the whole congregation of Israel." He sprinkled the throne of grace with the blood of a young bull and a goat, which he had previously to slaughter, and in this way absolved himself and his house "of the impurities of the sons of Israel and of their transgressions and of all their sins." No person was to be in the tent (i.e., in the holy place that lay in front of the Holy of Holies) when the high priest stepped into God's presence in this awesomely sacred place, this place where no one but he entered and he himself only at this hour. And even now he had to burn incense "so that a cloud of smoke . . . would veil the judgment throne . . . and he not die." This solitary dialogue took place in deepest mystery.

The Day of Atonement is the Old Testament antecedent of

Good Friday. The ram that is slaughtered for the sins of the people represents the spotless Lamb of God (so did, no doubt, that other — chosen by lot and burdened with the sins of the people — that was driven into the wilderness). And the high priest descended from Aaron foreshadows the eternal high priest. Just as Christ anticipated his sacrificial death during the last supper, so he also anticipated the high priestly prayer. He did not have to bring for himself an offering for sin because he was without sin. He did not have to await the hour prescribed by the Law, nor to seek out the Holy of Holies in the temple. He stands, always and everywhere, before the face of God; his own soul is the Holy of Holies. It is not only God's dwelling, but is also essentially and indissolubly united to God. He does not have to conceal himself from God by a protective cloud of incense. He gazes upon the uncovered face of the Eternal One and has nothing to fear. Looking at the Father will not kill him. And he unlocks the mystery of the high priest's realm. All who belong to him may hear how, in the Holy of Holies of his heart, he speaks to his Father; they are to experience what is going on and are to learn to speak to the Father in their own hearts.

The Savior's high priestly prayer unveils the mystery of the inner life: the circumincession of the Divine Persons and the indwelling of God in the soul. In these mysterious depths the work of salvation was prepared and accomplished itself in concealment and silence. And so it will continue until the union of all is actually accomplished at the end of time. The decision for the Redemption was conceived in the eternal silence of the inner divine life. The power of the Holy Spirit came over the Virgin praying alone in the hidden, silent room in Nazareth and brought about the Incarnation of the Savior. Congregated around the silently praying Virgin, the emergent church awaited the promised new outpouring of the Spirit that was to quicken it into inner clarity and fruitful outer effectiveness. In the night of blindness that God laid over his eyes, Saul awaited in solitary prayer the Lord's answer to his question, "What do you want me to do?" In solitary prayer Peter was prepared for his mission to the Gentiles. And so it has remained all through the centuries. In the silent dialogue with their Lord of souls consecrated to God, the events of church history are prepared that, visible far and wide, renew the face of the earth. The Virgin, who kept every word sent from God in her heart, is the model for such attentive souls in whom Jesus' high priestly prayer comes to life again and again. And women who, like her, were totally self-forgetful because of being steeped in the life and suffering of Christ were the Lord's preferred choice as instruments to accomplish great things in the church: a St. Bridget, a Catherine of Siena. And when St. Teresa, the powerful reformer of her order at a time of widespread falling away from the faith, wished to come to the rescue of the church, she saw the renewal of true interior life as the means toward this end. Teresa was very disturbed by the news of the continually spreading movement of apostasy:

> As though I could do something or were something, I cried to the Lord and begged him that I might remedy so much evil. It seemed to me that I would have given a thousand lives to save one soul out of the many that were being lost there. I realized I was a woman and wretched and incapable of doing any of the useful things I desired to do in the service of the Lord. All my longing was and still is that since he has so many enemies and so few friends that these few friends be good ones. As a result I resolved to do the little that was in my power; that is, to follow the evangelical counsels as perfectly as I could and strive that these few persons who live here do the same. I did this trusting in the great goodness of God.... Since we would all be occupied in continual prayer for those who are the defenders of the church and for preachers and for learned men who protect her from attack, we could help as much as possible this Lord of mine who is so roughly treated by those for

whom he has done so much good; it seems these traitors would want him to be crucified again....

O my Sisters in Christ, help me beg these things of the Lord. This is why he has gathered you together here. This is your vocation.

To Teresa it seemed necessary to use:

...the approach of a lord when in time of war his land is overrun with enemies and he finds himself restricted on all sides. He withdraws to a city that he has well fortified and from there sometimes strikes his foe. Those who are in the city, being chosen people, are such that they can do more by themselves than many cowardly soldiers can. And often victory is won in this way....

But why have I said this? So that you understand, my Sisters, that what we must ask God is that in this little castle where there are already good Christians not one of us will go over to the enemy and that God will make the captains of this castle, who are the preachers and theologians, very advanced in the way of the Lord. Since most of them belong to religious orders, ask God that they advance very far in the perfection of religious life and their vocation....

These persons must live among men, deal with men..., and even sometimes outwardly behave as such men do. Do you think, my daughters, that little is required for them to deal with the world, live in the world, engage in its business...while interiorly remaining its strangers...; in sum, not being men but angels? For if they do not live in this way, they do not deserve to be called captains; nor may the Lord allow them to leave their cells, for they will do more harm than good. This is not the time for seeing imperfections in those who must teach....

Is it not the world they have to deal with? Have no fear that the world will forgive this deficiency; nor is there any

> imperfection it fails to recognize. It will overlook many good things and perhaps not even consider them good; but have no fear that it will overlook any evil or imperfect things. Now I wonder who it is that teaches people in the world about perfection, not so much that these people might seek perfection . . . , but that they might condemn others. . . . So, then, do not think that little help from God is necessary for this great battle these preachers and theologians are fighting; a very great deal is necessary. . . .
>
> So, then, I beg you for the love of the Lord to ask His Majesty to hear us in this matter. Miserable though I am, I ask His Majesty this since it is for his glory and the good of the church; this glory and good is the object of my desires. . . .
>
> And when your prayers, desires, disciplines, and fasts are not directed toward obtaining these things I mentioned, reflect on how you are not accomplishing or fulfilling the purpose for which the Lord brought you here together.

What gave this religious, who had been living prayerfully in a monastery cell for decades, the passionate desire to do something for the church and the keen eye for the needs and demands of her time? It was precisely that she lived in prayer and allowed herself to be drawn ever more deeply by the Lord into the depths of her "interior castle" until she reached that obscure room where he could say to her, "that now it was time that she consider as her own what belonged to him, and that he would take care of what was hers." Therefore, she could no longer do anything more than "with zeal be zealous for the Lord, the God of Hosts" (words of our Holy Father, Elijah, which have been taken as a motto on the shield of the order). Whoever surrenders unconditionally to the Lord will be chosen by him as an instrument for building his kingdom. The Lord alone knows how much the prayer of St. Teresa and her daughters contributed to protect Spain from dissenting from the faith, and what power it exerted in the heated battles regarding the faith in France, the Netherlands, and Germany. Official history is silent about these invisible and incalculable forces. But they are recognized by the trust of the faithful and the carefully balanced judgment of the church after extensive investigations. And our time is more and more determined, when all else fails, to hope for ultimate salvation from these hidden sources.

Inner Life and Outer Form and Action

The work of salvation takes place in obscurity and stillness. In the heart's quiet dialogue with God the living building blocks out of which the kingdom of God grows are prepared, the chosen instruments for the construction forged. The mystical stream that flows through all centuries is no spurious tributary that has strayed from the prayer life of the church—it is its deepest life. When this mystical stream breaks through traditional forms, it does so because the Spirit that blows where it will is living in it, this Spirit that has created all traditional forms and must ever create new ones. Without him there would be no liturgy and no church. Was not the soul of the royal psalmist a harp whose strings resounded under the gentle breath of the Holy Spirit? From the overflowing heart of the Virgin Mary blessed by God streamed the exultant hymn of the Magnificat. When the angel's mysterious word became visible reality, the prophetic Benedictus hymn unsealed the lips of the old priest Zechariah, who had been struck dumb. Whatever arose from spirit-filled hearts found expression in words and melodies and continues to be communicated from mouth to mouth. The "Divine Office" is to see that it continues to resound from generation to generation. So the mystical stream forms the many-voiced, continually swelling hymn of praise to the triune God, the Creator, the Redeemer, and the Perfecter. Therefore, it is not a question of placing the inner prayer free of all traditional forms as "subjective" piety over against the liturgy as the "objective" prayer of the church. All authentic prayer is prayer of the church. Through every sincere prayer something happens in the church, and it is the church itself that is praying therein, for it is the Holy Spirit living in the church that intercedes for every individual soul "with sighs too deep for words." This is exactly what "authentic" prayer is, for "no one can say 'Jesus is Lord' except by the Holy Spirit." What could the prayer of the church be, if not great lovers giving themselves to God who is love!

The unbounded loving surrender to God and God's return gift, full and enduring union, this is the highest elevation of the heart attainable, the highest level of prayer. Souls who have attained it are truly the heart of the church, and in them lives Jesus' high priestly love. Hidden with Christ in God, they can do nothing but radiate to other hearts the divine love that fills them and so participate in the perfection of all into unity in God, which was and is Jesus' great desire. This was how Marie Antoinette de Geuser [French lay mystic, 1889–1918] understood her vocation. She had to undertake this highest Christian duty in the midst of the world. Her way is certainly a very meaningful and strengthening model for the many people who, having become radically serious about their inner lives, want to stand up for the church and who cannot follow this call into the seclusion of a monastery. The soul that has achieved the highest level of mystical prayer and entered into the "calm activity of divine life" no longer thinks of anything but of giving itself to the apostolate to which God has called it.

> This is repose in orderliness and, at the same time, activity free of all constraint. The soul conducts the battle in peace, because it is acting entirely from the viewpoint of eternal decrees. She knows that the will of her God will be perfectly fulfilled to his greater glory, because—though the human will often, as it were, sets limits for divine omnipotence—that divine omnipotence triumphs after all by creating something magnificent out of whatever material

> is left. This victory of divine power over human freedom, which he nevertheless permits to do as it pleases, is one of the most wonderful and adorable aspects of God's plan for the world....

When Marie Antoinette de Geuser wrote this letter, she was near the threshold of eternity. Only a thin veil still separated her from that final consummation that we call living in glory.

For those blessed souls who have entered into the unity of life in God, everything is one: rest and activity, looking and acting, silence and speaking, listening and communicating, surrender in loving acceptance and an outpouring of love in grateful songs of praise. As long as we are still on the way — and the farther away from the goal the more intensely — we are still subject to temporal laws, and are instructed to actualize in ourselves, one after another and all the members complementing each other mutually, the divine life in all its fullness. We need hours for listening silently and allowing the Word of God to act on us until it moves us to bear fruit in an offering of praise and an offering of action. We need to have traditional forms and to participate in public and prescribed worship services so that our interior life will remain vital and on the right track, and so that it will find appropriate expression. There must be special places on earth for the solemn praise of God, places where this praise is formed into the greatest perfection of which humankind is capable. From such places it can ascend to heaven for the whole church and have an influence on the church's members; it can awaken the interior life in them and make them zealous for external unanimity. But it must be enlivened from within by this means: that here, too, room must be made for silent recollection. Otherwise, it will degenerate into a rigid and lifeless lip service. And protection from such dangers is provided by those homes for the interior life where souls stand before the face of God in solitude and silence in order to be quickening love in the heart of the church.

However, the way to the interior life as well as to the choirs of blessed spirits who sing the eternal Sanctus is Christ. His blood is the curtain through which we enter into the Holiest of Holies, the Divine Life. In baptism and in the sacrament of reconciliation, his blood cleanses us of our sins, opens our eyes to eternal light, our ears to hearing God's word. It opens our lips to sing his praise, to pray in expiation, in petition, in thanksgiving, all of which are but varying forms of adoration, i.e., of the creature's homage to the Almighty and All-benevolent One. In the sacrament of confirmation, Christ's blood marks and strengthens the soldiers of Christ so that they candidly profess their allegiance. However, above all, we are made members of the Body of Christ by virtue of the sacrament in which Christ himself is present. When we partake of the sacrifice and receive Holy Communion and are nourished by the flesh and blood of Jesus, we ourselves become his flesh and his blood. And only if and insofar as we are members of his Body, can his spirit quicken and govern us. "It is the Spirit that quickens, for the Spirit gives life to the members. But it only quickens members of its own body.... The Christian must fear nothing as much as being separated from the Body of Christ. For when separated from Christ's Body, the Christian is no longer his member, is no longer quickened by his Spirit." However, we become members of the Body of Christ "not only through love..., but in all reality, through becoming one with his flesh: For this is effected through the food that he has given us in order to show us his longing for us. This is why he has submerged himself in us and allowed his body to take form in us. We, then, are one, just as the body is joined to the head." As members of his Body, animated by his Spirit, we bring ourselves "through him, with him, and in him" as a sacrifice and join in the eternal hymn of thanksgiving. Therefore, after receiving the holy meal, the church permits us to say: "Satisfied by such great gifts, grant, we beseech you, Lord, that these gifts we have received be for our salvation and that we never cease praising you."

—HL, 7–17

CONCERN FOR OTHERS

Edith Stein's commitment to furthering the world's well-being was nourished on the concept of vicarious suffering. This is reflected in the letter she sent to the Ursuline nun Mother Petra Brüning on December 9, 1938, just after the Kristallnacht pogrom and before her departure from Germany for then free Holland.

Cologne-Lindenthal, December 9, 1938

Dear Reverend Mother,

Many thanks for your loving letter of November 23. I must tell you that I already brought my religious name with me into the house as a postulant. I received it exactly as I requested it. By the cross I understand the destiny of God's people which, even at that time, began to announce itself. I thought that those who recognized it as the cross of Christ had to take it upon themselves in the name of all. Certainly, today I know more of what it means to be wedded to the Lord in the sign of the cross. Of course, one can never comprehend it, for it is a mystery....

And now I would like to wish you a very grace-filled Christmas feast. As the atmosphere around us grows steadily darker, all the more must we open our hearts to the light from above. Most cordial thanks once more for all the love you have shown me in these five years in the order. Since your way sometimes leads to Holland, I may even have the hope of seeing you again. I commend myself to your prayers for the next weeks and months.

In caritate Regis qui venturus est [in the love of the king who is to come] your grateful

Sister Teresa Benedicta of the Cross

—SPL, 295, 296

"TO STAND . . . FOR OTHERS"

In her desire to act as a leaven within the world, the operative word for Stein was "for." On the example of Christ she would live "for" the life of the world. She adopted terms similar to those of John's Gospel (6:51) in a letter sent on her last Christmas as a laywoman.

Dorsten, the second day of Christmas, 1932

Dear Anneliese,

. . . Before all else I would like to answer your question. There is a vocation to suffer with Christ and thereby to cooperate with him in his work of salvation. When we are united with the Lord, we are members of the Mystical Body of Christ: Christ lives on in his members and continues to suffer in them. And the suffering borne in union with the Lord is his suffering, incorporated in the great work of salvation and fruitful therein. That is a fundamental premise of all religious life, above all the life of Carmel, to stand proxy *for* sinners through voluntary and joyous suffering, and to cooperate in the salvation of humankind. [editor's italics]

With cordial wishes and greeting, your
Edith Stein

—SPL, 128

2

Letting God's Plan Guide Us

✝

The depth and breadth of St. Edith Stein's spiritual vision resist easy encapsulation, but she herself wrote that all her strivings could be summed up simply in the act of "living at the Lord's hand" (see the selection under this title). By that she meant that she stood ready to accept whatever came her way from God's kind disposition of events, from circumstances, and even from those initiatives by others that inescapably influenced her.

By her trusting adaptability she became a sign and source of hope for others, who often asked her for encouragement. A few months after arrival in Holland to begin her exile she counseled a young man looking forward to new employment in Nazi Germany: "Until then it means having patience and tarrying in the darkness.... So I too have to practice patience." In other words, he ought to believe that God's ever-present influence on people's lives would not let things slip through the cracks.

By relying on God, especially in moments of great difficulty or in answering calls for decisive action, Edith knew she could expect manageable outcomes from whatever she opted to do. A favorite scriptural summary of her basic spiritual attitude was Paul's comforting words in the Epistle to the Romans (8:28): "For those who love God, God makes all things turn out for their good." She sought no self-induced serenity, only the solid assurance of peace of mind that comes from seeking God's will in all things.

LILIES OF THE FIELD

To the biblical image of the lilies of the field and birds of the air Edith Stein juxtaposes the modern safeguard of insurance, thereby injecting a very modern twist to consideration of trust in God's providence.

To be a child of God means to go hand-in-hand with God, to do his will, not one's own; to place all our hopes and cares in his hands and no longer be concerned about one's self or future. Thereupon rest the freedom and the good cheer of the child of God. Yet how few of the truly devout, or even those truly heroic and willing to make sacrifices, possess them. They always go around bowed down under the heavy burden of their worries and responsibilities. They are all familiar with the parable of the birds in the sky and the lilies of the field [Matt. 6:26–34; Luke 12:24–31]. But whenever they encounter anyone who has no means, nor income, no insurance, and is none the less unconcerned about the future, then they shake their head, completely baffled.... Trust in God will remain unshakably firm only if it is willing to accept from the Father's hand anything and everything. He is the only one who knows what is good for us.... If this can be done, then one can freely live on for the present and for the future. —MC, 13–14

"A STATE OF RESTING IN GOD"

One striking note to this text is the fact it was written during Edith Stein's atheistic period, in 1919, several years before she accepted baptism.

Beyond these influxes of impulse power, which presuppose a certain amount of lifepower already — namely, that required for the experiencing of power-giving contents — there is obviously still another that isn't tied to that presupposition. There is a state of resting in God, of complete relaxation of all mental activity, in which you make no plans at all, reach no decision, much less take action, but rather leave everything that's future to the divine will, "consigning yourself entirely to fate." This state might have befallen me after an experience that exceeded my power, and that has completely consumed my mental lifepower and deprived me of all activeness. Compared to the cessation of activeness from the lack of lifepower, resting in God is something completely new and unique. The former was dead silence. Now its place is taken by the feeling of being safe, of being exempted from all anxiety and responsibility and duty to act. And as I surrender myself to this feeling, new life begins to fill me up, little by little, and impel me—without any voluntary exertion—toward new activation. This reviving infusion appears as an emanation of a functionality and a power which is not my emanation and which becomes operative within me without my asking for it. The sole prerequisite for such a mental rebirth seems to be a certain receptivity, like the receptivity supporting the structure of the person, a structure exempted from the sensate mechanism.

Something similar may be possible in the communications of one person with another. The love with which I embrace a human being may be sufficient to fill him with new lifepower if his own breaks down. Indeed, the mere contact with human beings of more intense aliveness may exert an enlivening effect upon those who are jaded or exhausted, who have no activeness as a presupposition on their side. I don't want to say anything more precise here about these relationships, which require their own study. They would be mentioned only because they serve to illuminate the sensate mechanism from a certain angle.

—PPH, 84–85

"ABLE TO REST IN GOD"

This advice on carrying out a day's activities in the light of God's intents and purposes took the form of a letter written to a group of working women living by a religious rule.

—St. Lioba, January 12, 1932

In the talk which I gave in November 1930 in Bendorf concerning the foundations of women's education, I tried to draw the picture of woman's soul as it would correspond to the eternal vocation of woman, and I termed its attributes as expansive, quiet, empty of self, warm, and clear. Now I am asked to say something regarding how one might come to possess these qualities.

I believe that it is not a matter of multiplicity of attributes which we can tackle and acquire individually; it is rather a single total condition of the soul, a condition which is envisaged here in these attributes from various aspects. We are not able to attain this condition by willing it; it must be effected through grace. What we can and must do is open ourselves to grace; that means to renounce our own will completely and to give it captive to the divine will, to lay our whole soul, ready for reception and formation, into God's hands.

Becoming empty and still are closely connected. The soul is replenished by nature in so many ways that one thing always replaces another, and the soul is in constant agitation, often in tumult and uproar.

The duties and cares of the day ahead crowd about us when we awake in the morning (if they have not already dispelled our night's rest). Now arises the uneasy question: How can all this be accommodated in one day? When will I do this, when that? How shall I start on this and that? Thus agitated, we would like to run around and rush forth. We must then take the reins in hand and say, "Take it easy! Not any of this may touch me now. My first morning's hour belongs to the Lord. I will tackle the day's work which he charges me with, and he will give me the power to accomplish it."

So I will go to the altar of God (Ps. 43:4). Here it is not a question of my minute, petty affairs, but of the great offering of reconciliation. I may participate in that, purify myself and be made happy, and lay myself with all my doings and troubles along with the sacrifice on the altar. And when the Lord comes to me then in Holy Communion, then I may ask him, "Lord, what do you want of me?" (St. Teresa). And after quiet dialogue, I will go to that which I see as my next duty.

I will still be joyful when I enter into my day's work after this morning's celebration: my soul will be empty of that which could assail and burden it, but it will be filled with holy joy, courage, and energy.

Because my soul has left itself and entered into the divine life, it has become great and expansive. Love burns in it like a composed flame which the Lord has enkindled, and which urges my soul to render love to inflame love in others: *flammescat igne caritas, accendat ardor proximos.* [Let charity be inflamed with fire, and ardor enkindle our neighbors.] And it sees clearly the next part of the path before it; it does not see very far, but it knows that when it has arrived at that place where the horizon now intersects, a new vista will then be opened.

Now begins the day's work, perhaps the teaching profession — four or five hours, one after the other. That means giving our concentration there. We cannot achieve in each hour what we want, perhaps in none. We must contend with our own fatigue, unforeseen interruptions, shortcomings of the children, diverse vexations, indignities, anxieties. Or perhaps it is office work: give and take with disagreeable supervisors and colleagues, unfulfilled demands, unjust reproaches, human meanness, perhaps also distress of the most distinct kind.

It is the noon hour. We come home exhausted, shattered. New vexations possibly await us there. Now where is the soul's morning freshness? The soul would like to seethe and storm again: indignation, chagrin, regret. And there is still so much to do until evening. Should we not go immediately to it? No, not before calm sets in at least for a moment. Each one must know, or get to know, where and how she can find peace. The best way, when it is possible, is to shed all cares again for a short time before the tabernacle. Whoever cannot do that, whoever also possibly requires bodily rest, should take a breathing space in her own room. And when no outer rest whatever is attainable, when there is no place in which to retreat, if pressing duties prohibit a quiet hour, then at least she must for a moment seal off herself inwardly against all other things and take refuge in the Lord. He is indeed there and can give us in a single moment what we need.

Thus the remainder of the day will continue, perhaps in great fatigue and laboriousness, but in peace. And when night comes, and retrospect shows that everything was patchwork and much which one had planned left undone, when so many things rouse shame and regret, then take all as it is, lay it in God's hands, and offer it up to him. In this way we will be able to rest in him, actually rest, and begin the new day like a new life.

This is only a small indication how the day could take shape in order to make room for God's grace. Each individual will know best how this can be used in her particular circumstances. It could be further indicated how Sunday must be a great door through which celestial life can enter into everyday life, and strength for the work of the entire week, and how the great feasts, holidays, and penitential times, lived through in the spirit of the church, permit the soul to mature the more from year to year to the eternal Sabbath rest.

It will be an essential duty of each individual to consider how she must shape her plan for daily and yearly living, according to her bent and to her respective circumstances of life, in order to make ready the way for the Lord. The exterior allotment must be different for each one, and it must also adjust resiliently to the change of circumstances in the course of time.

But the psychic situation varies with individuals and with each individual in different times. As to the means which are suitable for bringing about union with the eternal, keeping it alive or also enlivening it anew—such as contemplation, spiritual reading, participation in the liturgy, popular services, etc. — these are not fruitful for each person and at all times. For example, contemplation cannot be practiced by all and always in the same way.

It is important to each case to find out the most efficacious way and to make it useful for oneself. It would be good to listen to expert advice in order to know what one lacks, and this is especially so before one takes on variations from a tested arrangement. —EW, 143–45

"CARRIED BY A STRONG ARM"

Edith uses the wistful image of a child carried by its parent to raise an objection to Martin Heidegger's concept of human life as a process speeding onward grimly toward death.

Anxiety, to be sure, is under ordinary circumstances not the dominant mood of human life. It overshadows everything else only under pathological conditions, while normally we go through life almost as securely as if we had a really firm grip on our existence. This may in part be explained by the fact that we feel tempted to pause at any superficial view of life which simulates an appearance of lasting existence within a static temporal continuum and which under the veil of our multiple cares hides from us the sight of life's nullity. Generally speaking, however, this feeling of security in human existence cannot be called a mere result of such an illusion and self-deception. Any circumspect reflective analysis of the being of people shows clearly how little reason for such a feeling of security there is just in actual human existence, and to what extent the being of people is indeed exposed to nothingness.

Does this mean then that the feeling of existential security has been proven objectively groundless and irrational and that therefore "a passionate... consciously resolute and anxiety-stricken freedom toward death" represents the rational human attitude? By no means. The undeniable fact that my being is limited in its transience from moment to moment and thus exposed to the possibility of nothingness is counterbalanced by the equally undeniable fact that despite this transience, I am, that from moment to moment I am sustained in my being, and that in my fleeting being I share in enduring being. In the knowledge that being holds me, I rest securely. This security, however, is not the self-assurance of one who under her own power stands on firm ground, but rather the sweet and blissful security of a child that is lifted up and carried by a strong arm. And, objectively speaking, this kind of security is not less rational. For if a child were living in the constant fear that its mother might let it fall, we should hardly call this a rational attitude.

In my own being, then, I encounter another kind of being that is not mine but that is the support and ground of my own unsupported and groundless being. And there are two ways in which I may come to recognize eternal being as the ground of my own being. One is the way of faith when God reveals himself as he who is, as the Creator and Sustainer, and when our Redeemer says, "He who believes in the Son possesses eternal life" (John 3:36). Then I have in these pronouncements clear answers to the riddle of my own being. And when he tells me through the mouth of the prophet that he stands more faithfully at my side than my father and my mother, yea that he is love itself, then I begin to understand how rational is my trust in the arm that carries me and how foolish is all my fear of falling prey to nothingness — unless I tear myself loose from this sheltering hold.

The way of faith, however, is not the way of philosophic knowledge. It is rather the answer of another world to a question which philosophy poses. But philosophy has also its own specific way: It is the way of discursive reasoning, the way or ways in which the existence of God is rationally demonstrated.

—FEB, 55–57

"LIVING AT THE LORD'S HAND"

Loving acceptance of what comes to us from the "Lord's hand" sums up the spiritual vision of Edith Stein, and she uses this image often in her writings.

Breslau, April 28, 1931

Dear Sister Adelgundis,

You ask whether I have already begun my work. That happened at the end of January, two days after I returned from Freiburg, and in the six weeks in which I was still able to work in Speyer, a rather bulky manuscript materialized. At the same time it became clear that combining it with school and everything else was no longer possible. So, two and a half weeks before school ended, I arranged for another consultation with our Reverend Mother, and in full understanding of my situation, she released me. For the others it caused great consternation when, suddenly, on the last day of school, I said farewell. The children and most of the sisters had had no inkling beforehand. The few initiates helped me, with touching sisterly love, to complete the whole of my packing in the short time there was outside of school, so that I could escape to Beuron as soon as school closed....

Your criticism is not quite clear. It is, of course, true that the third part is not detailed enough. (The entire religious formation should have been included, as I once treated the matter in Munich.) But then, it appears that you did not want the supernatural to be brought up at all. But, if I could not speak about that, I would probably not mount a lecturer's platform at all. Basically, it is always a small, simple truth that I have to express: *How to go about living at the Lord's hand.* Then when people demand something else from me and propose very clever themes which are very foreign to me, I can take them only as an introduction in order to arrive eventually at my *ceterum censeo.* Perhaps that is a very reprehensible method. But my entire activity as lecturer has hit me like an avalanche, so that I have been unable as yet to reflect on it in principle. Most likely, I will have to do that some time.

In Beuron, I learned that a liturgical consultation is in the offing. I am glad that your way will now become clearer. With most cordial wishes for you and your work I am your

Edith

—SPL, 86–87

MY PLANS, GOD'S PLANS

The crucial words in this selection, "What did not lie in my plans, lay in God's plans," are not applied directly by Edith Stein to herself, but advance her thought in a hypothetical way. They oftentimes are cited to acknowledge how resilient she was in the face of abrupt shifts in her life.

The coherence of our own life is perhaps best suited to illustrate what we mean. In ordinary speech we distinguish between what is "planned" or "well-designed" — and this appears simultaneously as "meaningful" and "intelligible" — from what is merely "accidental" and which seems by itself meaningless and unintelligible. For example, I intend to pursue certain studies and to this end select a university which promised to provide some special incentive in my chosen field. Here we have a meaningful and intelligible coherence of motives and circumstances.

But the fact that in that particular university town I make the acquaintance of a person who is "accidentally" matriculated at the same institution and that one day I "accidentally" become engaged in talking on questions regarding an outlook on life — this seems at first glance hardly a thoroughly intelligible coherence of events. And yet when, many years later, I reflect upon my life, it becomes clear to me that this particular conversation turned out to be of decisive significance for my life, that it was perhaps more "essential" than all my studies so that now I am inclined to think that this encounter may have been "precisely the reason" why I "had to go" to that town. In other words, what did not lie in *my* plan lay in *God's* plans. And the more often such things happen to me the more lively becomes in me the conviction of my faith that — from God's point of view — nothing is *accidental,* that my entire life, even in the most minute details, was pre-designed in the plans of divine providence and is thus for the all-seeing eye of God a perfect coherence of meaning. Once I begin to realize this, my heart rejoices in anticipation of the light of glory in whose sheen this coherence of meaning will be fully unveiled to me.

—FEB, 109–10

"ABIDING IN HER PROVIDENCE"

Edith Stein felt early in life that she was destined to "be something great." Later on she realized providence was at work in all she had to face, so she pays tribute to the nourishing designs of God's providence in this text. She also uses a feminine attribution to God's Wisdom as it directs the providential plan of salvation and ends her thoughts with a quotation from Pseudo-Dionysius.

The *mixing bowl,* which Dionysius treats in his ninth letter, is also taken from the sapiential books. Holy Scripture says that kindly Wisdom brings a mysterious mixing bowl and offers the sacred drink it contains. But first she sets out solid food and raising her voice kindheartedly invites those who have need to drink. Divine Wisdom, then, serves two types of fare: solid, lasting food and liquid, flowing drink, and in the mixing bowl she shares her provident bounty. For the bowl, being round and uncovered, serves as a symbol of all-encompassing providence that at once penetrates and embraces everything. As the mixing bowl remains steady and solid, so providence goes forth to all things yet remains in herself, standing steadfast in her immovable sameness.

Now, Wisdom is said to build herself a house wherein she sets out solid food, cups, and a mixing bowl, so that it will be clear to anyone properly pondering godly things how for all things she is the perfect Originator of their being and welfare, goes forth to all, unfolds in the all, and encloses all things. However the same (Originator) is eminently in itself and in no wise in anything else. Rather, removed from everything, in itself it is the selfsame; it is, subsists, and remains in the same way and eternally, ever acting in the same manner, never going out of itself nor leaving its own abode, its immovable dwelling, its own hearth. But she (Wisdom), abiding therein (or in herself), accomplishes the entire, perfect work of providence, at once going forth to all yet abiding in herself, at once ever standing and moved yet not standing nor moved. Rather, so to speak, does she possess, at once in nature and above nature, the effect of her providence in abiding and her abiding in her providence.

> What then is the solid and liquid food? For goodly Wisdom is said to dispense and provide both at the same time. Solid food, I believe, stands for the spiritual, lasting perfection whereby in steady, powerful, uniform, undivided knowledge the spiritual senses of those to whom St. Paul, drawing from Wisdom, imparts truly solid food share in the divine. But liquid food, I think, refers to that far-

reaching, radiating teaching that endeavors to go forth to all things and leads its pupils by the good proportioned to them through the multiple, the diverse, and the divided to a simple and unwavering knowledge of God.

Spiritual and divine words are also compared to dew and water and to milk, wine, and honey as well, since like water they have the power to bring forth life, like milk to further growth, like wine to give renewed life, like honey to both purify and preserve. For divine Wisdom does bestow these things on her followers, granting them abundant and imperishable delights. And this is truly to feed; and hence Wisdom is praised both as giving life and nourishment and as giving new life and bringing about perfection.

—KF, 91–93

DISCERNING GOD'S DESIGNS

Edith Stein gives useful keys to discernment in the following words of advice and motivation. She reveals how much spiritual insight she derived from years of contact with the Benedictine monastic family.

The *Rule* of St. Benedict is called *discretione perspicua,* that is, distinguished by discretion. Discretion serves as a distinctive seal of Benedictine holiness. But fundamentally there is no holiness at all without it; indeed, if one grasps it with enough depth and breadth it becomes the same as holiness.

One entrusts a person with something "under discretion," that is, one expects silence to be kept about it. But discretion is more than keeping silence. A discreet person knows, without being requested to do so, when to refrain from speaking about something. He has the gift to *distinguish* between what must be kept in confidence and what must be revealed; when it is time to speak and when to be silent; *to whom* one may entrust something, to whom one may not. All this applies to his own affairs as well those of others. We do, after all, consider it an *indiscretion* if someone speaks about something concerning himself when it is untimely to do so, or when it would be harmful not to mention it.

One is handed a sum (of money) *at discretion,* that is, to be handled at our discretion. This does not imply we are to dispose of it at will. The donor has left us the choice of its application out of the conviction that we are most capable of deciding what should be done with it. In this case, too, discretion signifies a gift of discernment.

One who is to lead souls requires discretion to an exceptional degree. St. Benedict speaks of it when he enumerates what is required of the abbot (*Rule,* chap. 64). He should exercise "foresight and consideration," and distinguish whether he is imposing a divine or a worldly task; he is to *discern* and exercise judgment, mindful of Jacob's decision when he said: "If I demand too much from my herd on the way, they shall all die within a single day" (Gen. 33:13). This and other manifestations of *discernment,* the mother of virtues, the abbot should take to heart, weighing all things so as to attain that which the magnanimous require and from which the weak will not recoil in fright. One might render *discretio* here as "wise moderation." But the source of such wise moderation is, after all, the gift to discern what is to be required from every single person.

Where do we obtain this gift? To a certain degree, there is a natural disposition for it. This we call tact, or sensitivity, the fruit of an inherited spiritual culture and of wisdom which has been assimilated after much education and life experience. Cardinal Newman says that the perfect gentleman resembles the saint enough to be mistaken for one. But that can be so only until a certain test of strength occurs. Beyond this limit, such natural equanimity breaks down. Nor does natural discretion plumb any depths. True, this type of discretion knows how to "get along with people" and can function like machine oil lubricating the wheels of life in society. But the thoughts of the heart, the deep interior of the soul, remain hidden from it. Only the spirit penetrates that far, that Spirit who searches out all things, even the depths of divinity.

Genuine discretion is supernatural. It can be found only where the Holy Spirit reigns, where a soul listens in total surrender and unhampered flexibility to the soft voice of its fair Guest and awaits his least nod.

Is *discretio* to be considered a gift of the Holy Spirit? It is not to be taken for one of the well-known Seven Gifts of the Holy Spirit, nor is it a new eighth one. Discretion belongs essentially to each of the gifts: indeed, one could say that the Seven Gifts are varying expressions of this gift. The gift of fear distinguishes in God his Divine Majesty (*divina maiestas*) and measures the infinite distance between God's holiness and one's own impurity. The gift of piety distinguishes in God the benevolence (*pietas*) of his Fatherhood and looks to him with filial, reverential love, with a love that knows how to discern what is due to the Father in heaven.

In the gift of counsel, it is most obvious that it is a gift of making distinctions — distinguishing in every life situation what is the proper thing to do. In fortitude, one might be inclined to think that we are dealing solely with the matter of the will. But a distinction between "counsel" that recognizes the right path without taking it and a "fortitude" that blindly insists on its own way is possible only in the purely natural sense. Where the Holy Spirit reigns, the human spirit becomes docile and submissive. Counsel calls for uninhibited practical behavior; fortitude is enlightened by counsel. Together, they offer flexibility to the human spirit so it can make fitting adaptations to conditions. Because it submits to the Holy Spirit without resistance, it is capable of meeting any situation it confronts. This heavenly light, as the gift of knowledge, allows one to discern in all clarity everything created, and all that happens, according to its relation with the eternal order, to understand its structure, and to allot it its fitting place and the importance which is its due. Yes, as the gift of understanding, it gives one insight into the depths of Divinity itself, and allows revealed truth to shine forth in all its fullness. In its perfection as the gift of wisdom, it unites one with the Triune God, permitting one to plumb the meaning of the eternal Source of all which emanates from it and which is sustained by him in that divine movement of life which is recognition and love combined.

Accordingly, *sancta discretio* differs radically from human cleverness. It does not differentiate by thinking through a matter step-by-step as does the researching human spirit, nor by dissecting and reconstructing, not by comparison and gathering, nor through concluding and proving. It discerns as effortlessly as the human eye distinguishes the sharp outlines of things in full daylight. Penetrating into details does not cause it to lose sight of the connections that are to be seen in a comprehensive view. The higher a wanderer climbs, the wider the range of vision becomes, until the full panoramic view at the summit bursts forth. The spiritual eye, enlightened by the heavenly light, peers to the farthest reaches, blurs nothing, renders nothing indistinguishable. With this unity, fullness increases until in a single ray of divine light the whole world becomes visible, as happened for St. Benedict in the *magna visio*. —GL, 193–95

LED BY ANOTHER

The next selection recommends spiritual direction as a means to discovering God's plans for us. It makes the interesting suggestion that all "authentic" Catholics are destined to "become guides" of others.

Those who attain the freedom of these heights and expansive views have outgrown what is usually called "happiness" and "unhappiness." They may have to fight hard for worldly existence, may lack the support of a warm family life or, correspondingly, of the human community which sustains and supports — but lonely and joyless they can no longer be. Those who live with Holy Church and its liturgy, i.e., as authentic Catholics, can never be lonely: they find themselves embedded in the great human community; everywhere, all are united as brothers and sisters in the depths of their hearts. And because streams of living water flow from all those who live in God's hand, they exert a mysterious magnetic appeal on thirsty souls. Without aspiring to it, they must become guides of other persons striving to the light; they must practice spiritual maternity, begetting and drawing sons and daughters nearer to the kingdom of God.

The history of the church reveals that many persons, men and women, went this way "in the world." And, obviously, they are especially needed in our modern era. The modern pagan frequently finds every religious habit suspect and does not want to hear about any teaching of faith. This individual can scarcely even approach the supernatural life other than through persons he considers his worldly equal: those who perhaps practice the same profession, have strong common interests with the people of this world, and yet possess a mysterious power which comes from elsewhere.

A factor not yet mentioned is that in the lives of persons who have taken such an extraordinary path, we find, nevertheless, a general method: that of ascertaining God's will. This comes from obedience shown to a visible proxy of God — a priestly director. According to everything which we learn from personal experience and the history of salvation, the Lord's method is to form persons through other persons. Just as the child is assigned to the care and upbringing of an adult for its natural development, so also is the life of grace propagated through human mediation. Persons are used as instruments to awaken and nurture the divine spark. Thus, natural and supernatural factors reveal that even in the life of grace, "it is not good that the man should be alone."

Yet, at the same time, there is danger of self-deception: the spirit's clear glance is dimmed by the heart's wishes; consequently, a person is often confounded by mistaking for God's will that which suits his own inclination. In order to defend oneself from this danger, it is good to make decisions by submitting oneself to calm, unbiased judgment rather than by just following one's inner prompting. Another fact to be considered is that judgment in one's own affairs tends to be less certain and reliable than it is for others.

Along with these natural circumstances, there are connections to another order which doubtlessly have an even stronger effect. Each individual familiar with the interior life knows that it is precisely those called by God to achieve the extraordinary who must also pass through extraordinary tests. These are not only worldly difficulties and needs but rather spiritual suffering and temptations even harder to endure — that which mystical theology terms "the dark night of the soul." Although the purity of the will is not sullied, the soul falls into the utmost anxiety and confusion: it loses the taste for the practices of piety; it is tempted by skepticism and hostility toward ecclesiastical directives; it reaches the danger of considering its path to be a wrong one; it fears that it might be irrevocably lost.

Previous experience teaches that, in order not to lose the right way in the midst of such spiritual dangers, there is no better protection than obedience toward an enlightened religious director. It is *a mysterious* fact that obedience is efficacious against the powers of darkness — as is God's unique mercy in placing such a guide at the side of an afflicted soul — but it is a *fact.* God is not bound to this manner of mediation, but, for unfathomable reasons, he has so committed himself to us; similarly, he has also provided particular ways of intercessory grace, although his possibilities in working our salvation are endless. Inner and outer guidance must always go hand and hand on one's journey; for that reason, whoever finds the right spiritual director will allow himself, for his own good, to be led by God's guidance rather than by his own arbitrariness. To what functions this may destine individual persons only life itself can prove. —EW, 126–28

3

Searching for Deep Truth

✝

Edith cultivated an avid desire for learning which, from the beginning of her student days through to the end of her life, led her to search out the many facets of truth in all its complexity. Her own acute intelligence was an ever-present guide in her quest. She shared with her brother-in-law, Hans Biberstein, that characteristic which she termed "the questing nature of a researcher."

In all she attended three universities — Breslau, Göttingen, and Freiburg — moving from one major field of learning (psychology) to another (philosophy) to better satisfy her thirst for meaning. Her thesis, "On the Problem of Empathy," placed her among the leading proponents of phenomenology.

The choice of philosophy as her specialization reflected her desire for a tool of analysis capable of forging answers to the fundamental questions that intrigued her: What is the intimate nature of the things of this world and beyond it? What is the structure of the human person? How do persons establish and maintain communication with each other, with their communities, and other human groupings? What are their mutual roles in society?

Her choice of Edmund Husserl as a guide in her approach to these questions was significant. With phenomenology he had set going a new effort to break out of the subjectivist categories of idealism which dominated late nineteenth-century philosophy. Along with Husserl Edith sought after a truth that in later terms would be called "holistic" for its ability to embrace more than abstract formulae and to include consideration of values, emotions, and ultimate concerns such as peace and solidarity in the struggle for harmony and progress.

"EMPATHY AS THE UNDERSTANDING OF SPIRITUAL PERSONS"

The following passage is excerpted from her doctoral dissertation, "On the Problem of Empathy." While it was written by a person of no religious affiliation, the text shows how the author nevertheless let herself be led by phenomenology's openness to consider the behavior of believers (homo religiosus) *as a phenomenon worthy of consideration.*

I consider every subject whom I empathically comprehend as experiencing a value as a person whose experiences interlock themselves into an intelligible, meaningful whole. How much of this one's experiential structure I can bring to my fulfilling intuition depends on my own structure. In principle, all foreign experience permitting itself to be derived from my own personal structure can be fulfilled, even if this structure has not yet actually unfolded. I can experience values empathically and discover correlative levels of my person, even though my primordial experience has not yet presented an opportunity for their exposure. He who has never looked a danger in the face himself can still experience himself as brave or cowardly in the empathic representation of another's situation.

By contrast, I cannot fulfill what conflicts with my own experiential structure. But I can still have it given in the manner of empty presentation. I can be skeptical myself and still understand that another sacrifices all his earthly goods to his faith. I see him behave in this way and empathize a value experiencing as the motive for his conduct. The correlate of this is not accessible to me, causing me to ascribe to him a personal level I do not myself possess. In this way I empathically gain the type of *homo religiosus* by nature foreign to me, and I understand it even though what newly confronts me here will always remain unfulfilled. Again, suppose others regulate their lives entirely by the acquisition of material goods, allowing everything else to take second place, which I consider unimportant. Then I see that higher ranges of value that I glimpse are closed to them; and I also understand these people, even though they are of a different type.

Now we see what justification Dilthey has for saying, "The interpretive faculty operating in the cultural sciences is the whole person." Only he who experiences himself as a person, as a meaningful whole, can understand other persons. And we also see why Ranke would have liked to "erase" his self in order to see things "as they were." The "self" is the individual experiential structure. The great master of those who know recognizes in it the source of deception from which danger threatens us. If we take the self as the standard, we lock ourselves into the prison of our individuality. Others become riddles for us, or still worse, we remodel them into our image and so falsify historical truth.

—PE, 115–16

CONFRONTING BELIEFS

In the pursuit of truth one ought to adopt an active, critical stance. Edith here explains how it is important to confront beliefs, if only to avoid untruth. She stresses the characteristic working concept of phenomenology — to put aside assumptions — as a means of grasping a fuller knowledge of things and situations.

On the other hand, there exists a possibility that is not available with mere information. I can "take a stance" toward the attitude, in a new sense. I can accept it, plant my feet upon it, and declare my allegiance to it; or, I can comport myself negatively against it. Suppose I accept it — that means that if it emerges in me I give myself over to it, joyously, without reluctance. Suppose I deny it — that doesn't mean I eliminate it. That's not under my control. "Canceling out" a belief would require new motives, through which the motives of the original belief are invalidated and from which the cancellation is established instead "all by itself." But I need not acknowledge this belief. I can comport myself just as though it were not present; I can make it inoperative. (It is this, the comporting, that Husserl designated as *epoché*. The acts rendered inoperative are "neutralized.") For example, suppose I'm expecting a message that will oblige me to make a trip. Then I hear from an unreliable source that the event in question has taken place, and belief in it immediately imposes itself. But I "want" not to believe as long as I have no confirmed report. I comport myself just as I would if the belief were not present: I make no preparations, I go about my usual daily tasks, and so forth — nevertheless, the stance of belief is undeniably there.

As the following example shows, not only are certain actions abstained from (the "free" acts themselves), but rather the *epoché* can render the present attitude inoperative in actuality, so that even the — unfree — attitudes that it would have to evoke are discontinued. Suppose a mother hears from her son's buddies that he has died in the war. She's convinced that he's dead, but she "wants" not to believe it as long as she doesn't have the official report. For as long as she withholds her assent to the belief, the sorrow that would immediately develop from uninhibited belief doesn't awaken in her either. (This forestalling of sorrow by a neutralization of the motivating belief is, of course, basically essentially different from the struggle against sorrow when it imposes itself.) Or, suppose a convinced atheist is drawn into a religious experience of God's existence. He can't escape from the belief; but he doesn't plant his feet upon it, he doesn't allow it to become operative in himself, and he staunchly sticks with his "scientific worldview," which would be trashed by the unmodified belief. Or finally: Suppose somebody inspires my affection, and I can't prevent it. But I won't own up to it inwardly, and I withhold myself from it. That's completely different from the struggle against a tendency that you don't want to yield to. The struggle makes no sense at all as long as the inner consent isn't granted. If the tendency is made inoperative in this manner, then not only do I refrain from the actions that it would have to motivate, but involuntary expressions of a genuine inclination also cease of their own accord and don't even show up.

This adoption (or, denial) of an attitude, to which the attitude owes its character of being fully alive and operative (or, neutral), requires no independently executed act in order to exist; the attitude can emerge equipped with the one or the other from the start. But they could also be executed as acts in their own right at another time. However "free" I feel myself to be in this execution, it goes to show that I don't have the consciousness until right then to arouse the belief properly into life, but rather, as it were, I impart existence to the state of affairs that I believe in. In that I bestow unreserved belief on the report of a death, to me it's as though the event didn't happen until I made it happen irrevocably by my assent. As long as I refuse the assent, to me it's as though I still held fate at bay.

The counterpart to denial of a present attitude is adoption of one that's not present. I can plant my feet on a belief that in truth I do not possess and that is not alive within me. For example, I presume that I'm assessing the circumstances of my life sufficiently in order to be able to "make plans." Perhaps I resolve to take a trip next year, to move to another city, to finish up some work that I've begun, and so forth, and I arrange my present life entirely in regard to these future plans. However, deep down I am thoroughly convinced that some event is going to intervene that will trash all my plans. I deny my consent to this real live belief, and I don't let it become operative in me. The denial of an attitude is in every case equivalent to the adoption of a stance opposed to it; and the latter, although it is not a genuine living stance, now becomes determinative for my behavior subsequently.

Adoption and denial of attitudes have their motives and grounds, just as attitudes do. Motive and ground can coincide (as in the earlier cases). But they can also diverge. Suppose I refuse belief to a report because the messenger is untrustworthy. The untrustworthiness, and accordingly my knowledge of it, motivates and grounds my *epoché*, as it were. Or, I don't believe the report because it's unpleasant. The unpleasantness is my motive here, and the ground can be the same as before. However, it's also possible that my comportment [toward some attitude] is entirely without any objective ground. Where the two diverge or there's no ground at all, the attitude is an unreasonable one, and accordingly my comportment toward it, though free, is unintelligible.

It should be noted that in the field of information and attitude, a motive is never something irrelevant to rational grounding, something that lies beyond reason and unreason. In this sense, any motive has grounding power for a rational approach by the subject. Yet it can be that the subject makes a mistake in its approach; then it does something other than what is called for by the dominant motive. That which it does has its sufficient ground in a state of affairs that is not objective to the subject. In our example, the untrustworthiness is a rational motive of the *epoché*. The prejudice against it, which is called for by the *unacceptability* of the report, would be perhaps a defensive measure against what is reported. The *epoché* interpolates itself here as a surrogate for a functional defense. Such a "mistake" in approach, a sundering of motive and ground, takes place mainly when the motivation is not explicitly executed, and it can be unmasked by explication. Thus, implication is a source of deception and error; explication is the means to secure the supremacy of reason. Nevertheless, "irrational" motivations are possible only in the realm of reason. They are to be considered reason's fumbles. —PPH, 49–52

EMPATHY BRINGS COMFORT TO A FRIEND

In relating an incident during World War I Edith shows how well she used empathy as a key to the discovery of the truth of situations, no matter how intense.

...It was wonderful to climb the mountain in the evening, to wander about in the ancient castle, to think of Ekkehart [not Meister Eckhart] and of Schiller's youth, here where many a captive once languished in the fortress.

In the morning we were off to the lake. To the sound of church bells, an old woman ferried us in a rowboat from Radofzell to the island of Reichenau. The monastery made little impression on me on that occasion. Vineyards under a deep blue sky, the shimmering sunlight, and the lake's green waves lapping the shores—those are my most vivid recollections of that day.

But we came away with more than memories of happy outings, for impressions of a more serious nature were made, also [in Freiburg]. The first or second night after Erika's arrival there, we were awakened by an air raid. I was accustomed to that by this time and made little of it. Erika slept in another room; her bed was against the wall adjoining the room occupied by the landlady's elderly in-laws. During the night, suddenly, the man knocked at my door and told me in his Baden dialect that my companion was weeping. I dressed immediately and went over to her. She was, indeed, shedding tears but not for herself. She had been told that from Freiburg one could hear the artillery fire from the Vosges mountains and her brother Hans, a lieutenant, was stationed there.

Now she heard shells exploding and said, "If it sounds so terrible here, what a hell it must be there!"

I knelt beside her bed and comforted her. What we were hearing were the anti-aircraft guns from the *Schlossberg* which protected the entire city. All one could hear from the Vosges mountains was a very dull rumbling. Thereupon the tears stopped at once. Erika was completely comforted. She even noticed the dress I had thrown on so rapidly.

"You have found the style that suits you," she said.

—LJF, 406–7

EMPATHIC HELP FOR OTHERS

Ever the alert teacher, Edith Stein here describes her educational priorities. Imparting information or goals must always serve realistically to help the pupils, not aim blindly at fulfilling pre-established curriculum requirements.

College Marianum, Münster,
October 20, 1932

Pax!
Dear Sister Callista,

A distressing mound of letters has piled up for me in the last week — distressing, when one thinks of answering them. One wishes so much to send a word of thanks immediately, and yet I can only accomplish it very, very slowly. Now I am operating according to priority. Answer first those with urgent questions. Therefore you will receive a few lines so promptly.

Surely the children who attend convent schools should gain there the strength to form their lives in the spirit of Christ. Surely it is most important that the teachers truly have this spirit themselves and vividly exemplify it. At the same time they also need to know life as the children will find it. Otherwise there will be a great danger that the girls will tell themselves: "The Sisters have no notion about the world"; "They were unable to prepare us for the questions we now have to answer"; and the [danger is] that then everything might be thrown overboard as useless.

I have the impression that the Rhineland-Westphalian convents are more advanced in this (altogether the educational system here is decades ahead of the Bavarian one). You personally, though, have the advantage of not having entered too soon and of having belonged to the youth movement. That gives you access to much that others lack. However, it is necessary to keep up contacts. Today's young generation has passed through so many crises — it can no longer understand us, but we must make the effort to understand them; then perhaps we may yet be able to be of some help to them. There is not much use in recommending books to you since you do not have the time. But it seems to me you should be able to gain many an insight through your sister. Besides that, you probably have people come to consult you in the speakroom who see more of life than you do. And, of course, the children themselves bring in all sorts of things. All this has to be utilized.

As far as the faculty is concerned: I am convinced that it should be predominantly feminine. But *only* feminine? That I would not consider the ideal situation. In a family, it is also preferable if both father and mother are present and, together, bring up the children. There are paternal tasks a teacher has toward the girl students. Of course, it is preferable to have no male teachers than unsuitable ones. The same applies to the director. I consider a woman quite acceptable, but would not turn down a male just on principle. And if he were a skilled educator of girls — that is, one who at the same time is aware of the limits of his influence — then, where there is a *mixed* faculty it might be preferable.

Naturally I am also for a subject-oriented school system. I believe the weakness regarding education could be compensated if one had truly responsible "homeroom teachers" who gave as many courses as possible to their classes. If you teach German, history, and English to a class, you have enough opportunity to exercise an educational influence.

From the end of July to the beginning of September, I was in Breslau. The day before yesterday my mother had her 83rd birthday; things are still going well with her. My sister [Rosa] will have to continue to be patient. Please return Irmgard's letter at your convenience. I know nothing about an invitation to Mannheim.

Heartfelt thanks and best regards to your Mother Prioress.

All the best, your
Edith Stein

—SPL, 122–23

"DEEPER" IMPRESSIONS

Edith Stein would always appreciate the effect of art and architecture on the human spirit. The following passage shows how contact with religious depictions or structures left striking impressions destined to be reappropriated even more deeply in her later life.

Nor am I certain any more on which of the two trips I met Pauline Reinach in Frankfurt. We had a great deal to tell one another while we strolled through the old section of the city, so familiar to me because of Goethe's *Gedanken und Erinnerungen.*

But the deepest impressions were made on me by things other than the Römerweg and the Hirschgraben. We stopped in at the cathedral for a few minutes: and, while we looked around in respectful silence, a woman carrying a market basket came in and knelt down in one of the pews to pray briefly. This was something entirely new to me. To the synagogues or to the Protestant churches which I had visited, one went only for services. But here was someone interrupting her everyday shopping errands to come into this church, although no other person was in it, as though she were here for an intimate conversation. I could never forget that.

Later, Pauline led me along the River Main to the Liebig Institute where Myrion's *Athene* stands. But before we reached that statue we passed through a room where a sculptured group taken from a Flemish grave of the sixteenth century was displayed: the Mother of God, and John, in the center; Magdalen and Nicodemus on either side. There was no longer an image of Christ in the group. These figures had such an overpowering effect on us that, for a long while, we were unable to tear ourselves away. And as we went on from there to see the *Athene,* I found her very attractive but she left me cold. Only when I paid another visit there many years later was I able to appreciate her.

I also had an excellent guide in Heidelberg — Elisabeth Staiger, daughter of the Göttingen mathematician Felix Klein. I have probably already mentioned her as I got to know her at Reinach's at Christmastime, 1915. After her husband's death, she resumed teaching and was now employed here in a boys' school. She thoroughly enjoyed exchanging accounts with me of our experiences as teachers. I saw the Castle of Heidelberg, the Neckar, and, in the university library, the minnesingers' beautiful manuscripts. And, again, something other than any of these wonders of the world made a deeper impression on me: a "simultaneous" church, with a separating wall down its center. The church was used for services on one side by the Protestants and on the other by the Catholics. —LJF, 400–402

"ALL WHO SEEK TRUTH SEEK GOD"

This motto-like assertion about the importance of seeking the truth is so characteristic of Edith Stein that Pope John Paul II applied it to her in his homily of beatification on May 1, 1987. The letter is a touching instance of Christian grieving between two pupils, herself and Sr. Adelgundis Jaegerschmid, who was at the death-bed of Edmund Husserl, their beloved "Master" in phenomenology.

Cologne-Lindenthal, March 23, 1938

Pax Christi!
Dear Sister Adelgundis,

Our greetings go from one death-bed to the other. Our Sister Clara departed today for eternity, very gently, after a year of suffering. I commended our dear Master [Edmund Husserl] to her often, and will do so again tonight at the wake. I believe one is well taken care of in her company. She was our eldest lay sister, tireless in the lowliest of tasks, but a strong and manly character who had grasped and lived the Carmelite ideal with complete determination. So faith turned it into a completely spiritual life. I am not at all worried about my dear Master. It has always been far from me to think that God's mercy allows itself to be circumscribed by the visible church's boundaries. God is truth. All who seek truth seek God, whether this is clear to them or not. I am most grateful to you for every [bit of] news. April 21 will be my perpetual profession; on May 1, my Veiling.

After your letter of the 21st, I was able to ask the Sisters, as a community, to offer their Holy Communion for H. [Husserl] as a name day gift.

Most cordially, your
Teresa Benedicta a Cruce

—SPL, 272

"A YEARNING FOR UNVEILED CLARITY"

This passage proves the validity of Pascal's dictum in the voice of God: "You would not have sought me unless you had already found me." Edith Stein affirms here that grace is at work in all who sincerely seek after the Ultimate Meaning of their existence, even though they seem to be bereft of God.

We were attempting to show that in all genuine knowledge of God it is God himself who draws near the knower, although his presence may not always be felt as it is in experiential knowledge. In natural knowledge he draws near in images, works, and manifold effects; in faith by making himself known personally through the Word.

But in the case of any knowledge of persons, rather than disclosing oneself, one may *close* oneself—even withdraw behind one's own work. In this case the work still means something, retains an objective significance, but it no longer opens up access to the person, it no longer provides the contact of one mind with the other.

God wishes to let himself be found by those who seek him. Hence he wishes first to be sought. So we can see why natural revelation is not absolutely clear and unambiguous, but is rather an incentive to seek. Supernatural revelation answers the questions raised by natural revelation. Faith is already a finding and corresponds to God letting-himself-be-found, not only in the sense that he has something said about himself through his word but that through his word he himself has himself found.

Faith is a gift that must be accepted. In faith divine and human freedom meet. But it is a gift that bids us ask for more. As dark and lacking the evidence of insight, faith awakens a yearning for unveiled clarity; as mediated encounter it awakens a longing for an immediate encounter with God. Indeed the very content of faith awakens desire by promising the beatific vision.

On the other hand we can now see why God withdraws from those who fail to do his bidding to seek him, who remain apathetic in the face of the testimonies he gave of himself or who seek in them not God but means to their own ends, indeed even against God. God's word becomes a dead letter for the person who does not accept it as *God's* word. It no longer points beyond itself in a living way to the realm wherefrom it issues: the kingdom of the Divine Spirit. In many of its images, pagans may find confirmation of their idolatrous belief; dialecticians spot contradictions in different passages; moralists and educators disapprove of much it contains, since the hidden meaning is lost on them. —KF, 113–14

4

Woman and Women

Edith included in her autobiography the following epigram drafted to describe her main concerns as she entered the university:

Let woman equal be with man,
So loud this suffragette avers,
In days to come we surely can
See that a Cab'net post is hers.

While a university student Edith joined the Prussian Society for Women's Right to Vote. In those formative years and later on she welcomed opportunities to contribute to the promotion of women whenever they presented themselves.

As early as 1918 she protested the absence of women from university faculties within the jurisdiction of the Minister of Education for Prussia and received vindication from him when he wrote an advisory to university rectors that subsequently opened doors to positions for women teachers. The school in Speyer where she served as a lay teacher was a women's school. From there she was invited to give lectures on the place of women in society, the family, and in relation to men. She quickly became the brain trust of the Catholic women's movement in Germany during the 1920s because of her clear and cogent oratory.

Other productive women sought her advice and encouragement. Gertrud von le Fort visited her in Cologne Carmel and discussed with her the novella she wrote about the Carmelite nun martyrs of Compiègne under the French Terror, Song at the Scaffold. *Von le Fort said she thought of Edith Stein often as she developed her volume* The Eternal Woman: *"I kept calling to mind my picture of Edith Stein which seemed to embody for me what I wished to portray as 'a truly Christian woman.'"*

Despite distance and, later, her cloistered life Edith maintained a wide network of women friends, and in her correspondence with them she often offered insight into the personal and general problems of women. Most of her writings on the theme of woman were first delivered as lectures, but other writings afforded her the chance to develop variations on the theme. In declaring her co-patroness of Europe (along with St. Bridget of Sweden and St. Catherine of Siena, both saints of the Middle Ages) Pope John Paul II took special note of her writings about the role and contribution of women in the modern world.

WOMAN'S INTRINSIC VALUE IN NATIONAL LIFE

Several organizations promoted Edith's career as an international lecturer by inviting her to explain her thought on women's issues. This is the full text of a talk she gave on April 12, 1928, at Ludwigshafen on the Rhine to the fifteenth convention of the Bavarian Catholic Women Teachers Association.

Honored guests, dear colleagues.

Please let me begin with a short personal observation. Two days ago, I traveled from Beuron, where I was permitted to spend Holy Week and Easter Sunday, to Ludwigshafen into the midst of preparation for the convention. One can hardly imagine a greater contrast: there, the quiet valley of peace where, unconcerned with everything that happens abroad in the world, praise to the Lord is sung day after day, year after year *a custodia matutina usque ad noctem* and this assembly which has gathered to speak of burning contemporary questions.

This was almost like dropping from heaven to earth. But perhaps this contrast is a direct symbol of the problem which we all have. Within the last week, we have all gone the way of the cross with our Savior; all our hearts still exult in the paschal Alleluia. And in a week we must return to our ordinary duties. But the efficacy of the Passion and Easter should not be an incidental holiday disposition dissipated by ordinary life; on the contrary, it is a living power of God within us which we interweave into our professional life. And this convention ought to help us to do so.

Now to the topic. For me, this topic in its precise working indicates how much the image of the feminist movement has changed recently. Even twenty years ago, it would have scarcely occurred to anyone to pose such a question. The big slogan in the beginning of the feminist movement was *Emancipation.* That sounds rather lofty and revolutionary: liberation from the chains of slavery. The demands were more practical: removal of the fetters which prevented women from entering into the same educational and professional activities *as men.* Woman's personal capabilities and powers, often dwarfed without these opportunities for action, were to be liberated. Hence the goal was one of *individualism.* Outside the extreme left, this demand met lively resistance. "Woman's place is in the home!" resounded from every side. It was feared that granting women's demands would jeopardize feminine singularity and woman's natural calling. On the other hand, these opponents maintained that woman was not qualified for *masculine* professions because of her singularity. The Suffragettes violently opposed this view; and, in the heat of battle, they went so far as to *deny* completely the feminine *singularity* — that women were any different from men. Consequently, one could not speak of an intrinsic *feminine value.* (As a matter of fact, their only goal was to insist that women were equal to men in all fields.)

The Weimar Constitution recognized women's claims to such a degree that the most audacious pioneers of the feminist movement would not have believed it possible for it to take place so soon. And with that a change commenced. The heat of battle cooled. One was again capable of judging calmly and clearly. Besides, today we can speak from years of experience concerning the future of the professional woman; whereas earlier, the arguments of both factions were *a priori* judgments, if not completely arbitrary ones. So the contemporary situation is characterized primarily by feminine *singularity* being accepted as *self-evident.* We women have become aware once again of our singularity. Many a woman who formerly denied it has perhaps become aware of it, painfully aware of it, if she has entered one of the traditionally masculine professions and sees herself forced into conditions of life and work alien to her nature. If her *nature* is strong enough, she has perhaps succeeded in converting the *masculine* profession into a *feminine* one. And this *self-awareness* could also develop the conviction that an *intrinsic feminine value* resides in the singularity.

And finally, a contemporary trend became decisive for the acceptance of feminine singularity also. The individualistic disposition of the nineteenth century has yielded more and more to a social disposition. Today, that which is to be of value must be made fruitful for the community. And our theme upholds that this possibility also exists for the intrinsic value of woman.

The first task now is to sketch briefly the *singularity* of women, for it is indeed only by doing this that the intrinsic value can be made comprehensible. During the last few decades, psychology has been much occupied with the psychical differences between the sexes; certainly, experiment and statistics revealed much more than what ordinary experience already teaches. I would like to emphasize only two criteria differentiating man from woman from those which are usually mentioned, since they have particular significance in helping us understand the intrinsic value of woman.

1. Man appears more *objective:* it is natural for him to dedicate his faculties to a discipline (be it mathematics or technology, a trade or business management) and thereby to subject himself to the precepts of this *discipline. Woman's attitude is personal;* and this has several meanings: in one instance she is happily involved with her total being in what she does; then, she has particular interest for the living, concrete person, and, indeed, as much for her own personal life and personal affairs as for those of other persons.

2. Through submission to a discipline, man easily experiences a *one-sided development.* In woman, there lives a natural drive toward *totality* and *self-containment.* And, again, this drive has a twofold direction: she herself would like to become a *complete human being*, one who is fully developed in every way; and she would like to help others to become so, and by all means, she would like to do justice to the complete human being whenever she has to deal with persons.

Both of these characteristic impulses as they *emerge from nature* do not demonstrate yet any initial value; indeed, they can be harmful. But, correctly handled, they can become most valuable. Let us clarify the *value of the personal attitude and the tendency to completeness*, and then consider how this value can be developed from the raw material.

The personal attitude is objectively justified and valuable because actually the human person is more precious than all objective values. All truth is discerned by persons; all beauty is beheld and measured by persons. All objective values exist in this sense for persons. And behind all things of value to be found in the world stands the *person of the Creator* who, as prefigurement, encloses all earthly values in himself and transmits them. In the area of our common experience, the human being is the highest among creation since his personality is created in the image of God. It is the *whole person* about whom we are speaking: *that* human being in whom God's image is developed most purely, in whom the gifts which the Creator has bestowed do not wither but bloom, and in whom the faculties are balanced in conformity to God's image and God's will — the will led by intellect, and the lower faculties bridled by intellect and will.

Each human being is called naturally to this total humanity, and the desire for it lives in each one of us. We may consider that the drive for this which is particularly strong in woman is well related to her particular destiny of companion and mother. *To be a companion,* that means to be support and mainstay, and to be able to be so, a woman herself must stand firmly; however, this is possible only if inwardly everything is in right order and rests in equilibrium. *To be a mother* is to nourish and protect true humanity and bring it to development. But again, this necessitates that she possess true humanity herself, and that she is clear as to what it means; otherwise, she cannot lead others to it. One can become suitable for this double duty if one has the *correct personal attitude.* As we have already stated, woman does not possess this by nature. The initial form of feminine singularity is primarily a debasement and blockage of this true attitude. On the one hand, it is a bias *to secure her own personal importance* by which she may busy herself and others; also, it is an inability to endure criticism which is experienced as an attack on her person. These yearnings for importance, yearnings toward unlimited recognition, are extended to everything unique to the person. Her own husband must be recognized as the very best husband, her own children must be known as the most beautiful, clever, and gifted. This is blind feminine love which dulls realistic judgment and renders her completely unsuitable for the designated feminine vocation. Along with this excessive vindication of her own person goes an *excessive interest in others*, a perverse desire to penetrate into personal lives, a passion of wanting to confiscate people. Excess of interest in both her own and in the stranger's personality merge in feminine surrender, the urge to lose herself completely in a human being; but in so doing, she does justice neither to self nor to the humanity of another, and, at the same time, becomes unfit for exercising other duties.

Also connected to the false pursuit of prestige is a perverted desire for totality and inclusiveness, a mania to know everything and thereby to skim the surface of everything and to plunge deeply into nothing. However, such superficiality can never be true humanity. Whoever controls a matter thoroughly stands closer to true humanity than he who never stands on firm ground. Among those who have a thoroughly objective formation, there are certainly more men than women. However, in the *small flock* that approaches the goal of full humanity there seem to be more women than men.

How is it then possible to extricate the purified valuable feminine character from the raw material of feminine singularity with all its faults and weaknesses, of which, as daughters of Eve, we all have a share?

In the first instance, a good natural method for this is *thoroughly objective work*. Every such work, no matter of what kind, whether housework, a trade, science, or anything else, necessitates submitting to the laws of the matter concerned; the whole person, thoughts just as all moods and dispositions, must be made subordinate to the work. And whoever has learned this, has become *objective,* has lost something of the *hyper-individuality* and has attained a definite freedom of self; at the same time she has attained an inner depth — she has attained a basis of self-control. Indeed, every young girl should receive a basic vocational formation for the sake of these great personal gains, quite aside from any economic compulsion; and after this formation, she should hold a position which completely fulfills her. No other environment than the life of the *high school* girl of the old style and that of the unoccupied woman from affluent circles provides a more fertile soil for the debasement of the feminine singularity and for hysteria, its sickly enhancement. Because objective work, which we view as a remedy for the faults of feminine singularity, is something to which the average man is naturally inclined, it can thus be said as well that an allowance of masculine nature is the antidote for the *hyper-feminine nature*. But with this, we in reality propose that, after all, the matter cannot rest there. It would be to attain thereby only an analogy to the masculine species, as, in fact, it frequently was in the beginning of the feminist movement; and that would be neither a greater gain for us nor for others. We must advance further from the objective outlook to the proper personal one, which is also the attitude that is actually most highly objective. But relevant to this personal outlook is a realization of true humanity, i.e., of its ideal image, and a perception of the predispositions toward it as well as departures from it within ourselves and in others, a freedom of insight, an autonomy within ourselves and in others, and a power for enforcement of the needed practical precautions that cannot win at all by human means. No book learning can give this acuteness of vision to our blind sight, no straining of the will can provide the energy to clip the wild shoots within ourselves and in those people dear to us. Supernatural means must now come to our help.

To begin with, where do we have the concrete image of total humanity? God's image walked among us in human form, in the Son of Man, Jesus Christ. If we reflect on how this image speaks to us in the simple account of the Gospels, it then opens our eyes. The better we get to know the Savior, the more we are conquered by his sublimity and gentleness, by his kingly freedom which knows no other obligation than submission to the Father's will, and by his freedom from all living creatures which is simultaneously the foundation for his compassionate love toward each living creature. And the deeper this image of God penetrates into us, the more it awakens our love. In just this way, we become the more sensitive to all falling away from him in ourselves and in others; our eyes are opened, free of all extenuations, to true knowledge of human nature. And if the power fails us to endure the sight of human weakness in ourselves and in others, only a look at the Savior is again needed; indeed, he has not turned from our misery with horror, but he came to us exactly because of this misery and took it upon himself — *vere languores nostros ipse portavit et livore eius nos sanati sumus.* Thus he himself has the remedy if we do not know where to find redress. Through his sacraments, he purifies and strengthens us. And if we turn confidently to him, which is his will, his spirit penetrates us more and more and converts us; through union with him, we learn to dispense with human props and to gain the freedom and strength which we must have in order to be the support and mainstay for others. He himself guides us and shows us how we should guide others. We therefore achieve total humanity through him and, simultaneously, the right personal attitude. Whoever looks to him and is concentrated on him sees God, the archetype of all personality and the embodiment of all value. The surrender to which feminine nature inclines is here appropriate; on the other hand, we also *find* here the absolute love and surrender for which we seek vainly in people. And surrender to Christ does not make us blind and deaf to the needs of others — on the contrary. We now seek for God's image in each human being and want, above all, to help each human being win his freedom. Accordingly, we can now also say: the *intrinsic value of woman* consists essentially in *exceptional receptivity for God's work in the soul*, and this value comes to unalloyed development if we abandon ourselves confidently and unresistingly to this work.

Only now have we come to the second part of our theme — the significance of woman for national life. This significance presents itself as a simple conclusion from what has been said. What is, then, the great sickness of our time and of our people? There is an inner disunion, a complete deficiency of set convictions and strong principles, an aimless drifting. Therefore, the great mass of humanity seeks for an anesthetic in ever new, ever more refined delights. Those who wish to maintain a sober level of life, in order to protect themselves from contemporary turmoil, frequently annihilate this level by one-sided professional work; but even they cannot do anything to escape the turmoil. Only whole human beings as we have described them are immune to the contemporary sickness: such beings are steadfast on eternal first principles, unperturbed in their views and in their actions by the changing modes of thoughts, follies, and depravities surrounding them. Every such individual is like a pillar to which many can fasten themselves, thereby attaining a firm footing. Consequently, when women themselves are once again whole persons and when they help others to become so, they create healthy, energetic spores supplying healthy energy to the entire national body.

They are able to do this above all in their vocation as *mother*. These are mothers who have a firm philosophy of life, who know to *what purpose* they should rear their children, who have an open vision of the developmental possibilities of their children. But also they have an incorruptible perspective of the dangerous drives in them which must be curtailed and which must be seized with a powerful hand at the right moment. And these also must be mothers who know their place, who do not think that they are able to do everything themselves but, on the contrary, are able to let go of their children and place them in God's hand when the time comes, when the children have outgrown them. Such mothers are probably the most important agents for the recovery of the nation. Also, woman frequently has the duty to help all humanity toward victory in relation to her spouse. He generally has the need "to be an individual also" when he comes from his professional activity, but often he no longer has the strength to be able to do so on his own. The wife's concern must therefore be to take care that he does not look for compensation in shallow or dangerous diversions. A fine home creates an atmosphere in which the soul can freely breathe. And then the values which she longs for are materialized naturally. Tact and delicacy must discover what is to be settled at a given moment. Often the proper relationship between the father and children, which is of greatest significance for both parties, must above all be mediated by the mother. And in countless cases, it is the difficult, thorny duty of the woman to win back to the faith a husband who is indifferent to religion or who rejects it. This is a task of greatest responsibility which only very few — even with proper good will — know how to handle in the right way. For here, in most cases, more is lost rather than gained by much talk or even with scolding. Even in apparently desperate cases, weapons which have led to victory are to go one's own quiet and unperturbed path (along with the greatest of all loving cooperation and civility), and, in self-surrender, to pray constantly. The battle is not always won, for here it is a question of God's mystery which we cannot penetrate.

Close to that of spouse and mother, the profession of *teacher* has always been valued as a truly feminine vocation. The teacher certainly has to shape mankind. And in our times in which the home breaks down so frequently, the future of our people depends more than ever on the teaching body. And with this comes a grave responsibility. Certainly, the school in many instances can no longer rectify the wrongs committed in the home. But it must try to do this by every means. And today, when we recognize at last that the primary school must be the training school of our people, we may hope that by degrees this will also be accomplished in the high schools as well, and that the curricula will undergo the necessary reshaping and improvement in order to free forces for the educational task of the school. And what is efficacious for the mother is naturally efficacious for the educator as well, and in an enhanced degree. She must *be firm:* confusion in young heads and hearts is produced by wobbly and untested perspectives, by undigested and indigestible fruits of reading, a confusion which many times can be remedied no longer. And particularly when the teacher has to deal with older children, her theoretical basis must be well grounded because she will meet interferences and objections which occur less frequently at home. The teacher thus needs a basic education in dogma and asceticism. Apologetics is certainly also good, but the former seems more important to me: ready arguments, as right as they may be, often do not have penetrating force. But she whose soul is formed through the truths of faith — and I call this ascetic formation — finds words which are proper for *this* human being and for *this* moment respectively.

And in one respect the teacher has it more difficult, for the natural bond of love which exists between mother and child from the beginning does not exist between her and the children. Love and trust are, however, necessary rudiments for every educational influence in depth. On the part of the teacher, this love and trust must be won by means of a nature which loves consistently. And truly supernatural forces are needed to offer such equal, motherly love to *all*, even to the unlovable, the difficult, the intolerable children — and especially to them because, indeed, they are in most need of it.

Woman's vocation as teacher has never been disputed. But even other professions, which were considered earlier as masculine monopolies, have changed through usage and have shown themselves in keeping with feminine individuality; these professions are so constituted that they can be mastered through truly feminine handling, in the right sense. I am thinking of the profession of the medical woman. I have made the gratifying observation that women who have once been in the care of a woman doctor do not willingly give themselves again to other treatment. It may be that a feeling of shame contributes to this fact. But I believe that something else is even more important. As a rule, the sick who visit or send for a doctor do not seek merely to have a particular organ healed of a particular trouble; one feels himself "out of line" in his entire system;

one seeks healing for body and soul, and one also desires a friendly, comprehensive sympathy. This was to be found in the house doctor of the old school. But this beneficial service has become just about extinct, ousted through specialization. This development naturally cannot be revoked. Medical science has adopted such proportion that it is no longer actually possible to master fundamentally all its divisions. But in specialization it should not be forgotten that in most cases it is not only the organ but, on the contrary, it is the entire person who is sick along with the organ. Just as in the knowledge of the illness, so is it also not a matter of indifference as to what kind of person the doctor is facing in regard to the medical treatment. The symptoms are not exactly the same with each individual, and even much less can every remedy be of value for each one. And, as we have said, it is, moreover, consideration of the whole being which approaches the spiritual needs of the sick person. As we have seen, such a regard lies in the nature of woman. And if she exercises her medical vocation in this manner, she can thus attain much more than healing the actual illness. She receives insight into diverse human situations; she necessarily gets to see material and moral need. This is a wide area for authentic feminine activity, and it signifies Christian charity at the same time.

We have arrived at the large range of social vocations which have in most part been formed only in recent years or are still in the process of formation. They all require womanly hands and, naturally, also women who are whole persons: the vocations of social worker, welfare worker for young people, nursery school teacher, administrator in a jail or factory, etc. Everywhere, the problem is to save, to heal endangered or demoralized humanity, to steer it into healthy ways. In order not to anticipate later papers, I do not want to examine these vocations more closely here. I do want to say only a few words on scholarly work for women because you perhaps expect something from me precisely on that subject. I believe that in reality there is less occasion here for the effect of feminine intrinsic value. Scholarship is the realm of the most austere objectivity. Hence, feminine singularity will only fructify where the subject deemed worthy of research is in a personal direction, i.e., in the humanities: history, literature, etc. Whoever chooses one of the abstract sciences — mathematics, natural sciences, pure philosophy, etc. — finds that as a rule, the masculine-intellectual type predominates in at least whatever is related to pure research. However, woman may perhaps assert her singularity anew in such areas of knowledge by the way she instructs; this is a helpful way which brings her into close relationship with people.

In addition, I would like to speak of the intrinsic value of woman in *political life*. In *legislation,* there is always danger that resolution "at the official level" will be based on the elaboration of the possibly most perfect paragraphs without their consideration of actual circumstances and consequences in practical life. Feminine singularity resists this abstract proceeding; woman is suited to act in accordance with the concrete human circumstance, and so she is able to serve as redress here. She has also already proved herself as a blessed counterbalance against another deterioration of *masculine objectivity*. The intention of the politician's party is often the *object* which is of primary importance for him, one to which he has dedicated himself. And somehow, this can result in the highest unobjectivity by the manipulation of a bill's draft. Thus, years ago on the deliberation of youth laws, the danger did exist that the project would end in failure by party opposition. The women of the differing parties at that time worked together and reached an agreement. The authentic feminine longing to remedy human need was thus victorious over the dilemma of party viewpoint. Just as in legislation, feminine singularity can also work beneficially in the application of the law in *bureaucracy,* provided it does not lead to abstract validation of the letter of the law but to the accomplishment of justice for humanity.

Finally, woman's intrinsic value can work in every place and thereby institute grace, completely independent of the profession which she practices and whether it concurs with her singularity or not. Everywhere she meets with a human being, she will find opportunity to sustain, to counsel, to help. If the factory worker or the office employee would only pay attention to the spirits of the persons who work with her in the same room, she would prevail upon trouble-laden hearts to be opened to her through a friendly word, a sympathetic question; she will find out where the shoe is pinching and will be able to provide relief. Everywhere the need exists for maternal sympathy and help, and thus we are able to recapitulate in the *one* word *motherliness* that which we have developed as the characteristic value of woman. Only, the motherliness must be that which does not remain within the narrow circle of blood relations or of personal friends; but in accordance with the model of the Mother of Mercy, it must have its root in universal divine love for all who are there, belabored and burdened.

Thus I can summarize that a high vocation is designated in feminine singularity—that is, to bring true humanity in oneself and in others to development. But hazardous germs also lie in feminine singularity which endanger the essential value in its development and thereby the realization of mission. The dangers can only be conquered through rigorous discipline in the school of work and through the liberating power of divine grace. Our mission is to become flexible instruments in God's hand and to effect his work to which he leads us. If we fulfill our mission, we do what is best for ourselves, for our immediate environment, and together with it, what is best for the entire nation.

—EW, 253–65

"TO KNOW AND UNDERSTAND THE WORLD AND PEOPLE"

From a longer essay, "Principles of Women's Education," this segment discusses an ideal balance among values, reason, and faith in the education of young women.

We see that the possibility exists of the inner formative functions needing the help of exterior ones; indeed, that is the hypothesis of all education. Formal education enhances the development of the given physical and intellectual *organs,* and it produces suitable educational material. Both work extensively together. Trained functions are needed for the reception of the materials; on the other hand, these functions can only be trained by material. The treatment of the body belongs naturally in an integral theory of women's education. I leave it to the experts to deduce the natural educational work provided by anatomy and physiology; I wish only to investigate education in respect to the soul. What materials does the soul need for its development? It must receive something into itself in order to grow. And, as we have seen, only that which the soul receives *internally* can become an integral part of it so that we can speak of growth and formation; that which is received by senses and intellect remains an exterior possession. We call *qualities* the objects which have something in themselves which make them fit for reception into the interior of the soul; we call this something itself *value.*

An especially strong natural desire for such spiritually nourishing values lives within the soul of woman. She is predisposed to love the beautiful, inspired by the morally exalted; but, above all, she is open to the highest earthly values, the inexpressible ones that remain in the essence of the souls themselves. It was thus undoubtedly legitimate when *emotionally formative* subjects — literature, art, history — occupied an extensive place in the education of girls until a few years ago. I quite believe that, in the former period, at least the more gifted girls of the often-derided *Höheren Töchterschule* profited by a good share of effectual education.

Yet the fact that emotionally formative material is generally received is of less importance; such material must become assimilated in the right way, thereby cooperating in formation. There is a law that rules this formation — the law of *reason.* The respective place in the soul to be reasonably yielded to values and qualities corresponds to the structure of the external world and to its gradation of these values and qualities. In order that the soul be rightly formed and not malformed, it must be able to compare and discriminate, weigh and measure. It may not be impregnated with an equivocal enthusiasm; it may not be filled with fanaticism; and it must attain fine perception and sharp judgment.

A well-developed intellect pertains to that end. Even if abstract intellectual activity is on average less suited to women, the intellect is nevertheless the key to the kingdom of the mind; it is the eye of the mind, and through it light penetrates into the darkness of the soul. In her Graz address on "Woman's Mission," Oda Schneider said that it suffices for women to live and not to ask a protracted "what" and "to what purpose." But in that lies the strong danger of error, of loss of purpose and aim. The significance of masculine control was elucidated in that address. But that should not mean the relinquishing of one's own judgment in favor of dependence. The intellect, which for all that is surely *there*, may and must be moved to action. It cannot, by any means, become lucid and acute enough. But, of course, the development of intellect may not be increased at the expense of the refinement of emotion. That would mean turning the means into the end. The main point is not to admit into the curriculum *everything* recommendable as purely intellectual training. It would be advisable, on the contrary, if the trouble were taken to achieve a maximum result with a minimum expense so that the greatest possible opportunity remains for material improvements.

Moreover, one must remember that there is not only a theoretical but also a practical intelligence which is faced in daily life by the most diverse tasks. It is, first of all, of extraordinary importance for later life to train this faculty; and it is formed through exercise in concrete tasks, not in theoretical problems. It suits the nature of woman better because she is indeed more oriented to the concrete than to the abstract. And along with it should go schooling of the will from which achievements are constantly asked: choice, judgment, renunciation, sacrifice, etc. And training of the practical intellect is also essential for the cultivation of proper emotions. Only where conviction and intention are successfully translated into action can it be shown whether an enthusiasm is legitimate, whether higher things are actually preferred over lower things. Finally, human nature is geared not only toward receiving but also toward acting by giving shape to the external world.

For that reason, an essential part of the educational process is the activation of one's practical and creative capacities. And practical abilities in life are required of the majority of women. Only if we have allowed them to already *act* during the time of schooling will we rear practical, able, energetic, determined, self-sacrificing women.

Several basic points of reference for an *educational plan* now emerge as exacted by the nature and vocation of woman. One would have to be entirely free of the notion that schooling should give a compendium of all the areas of knowledge of our time. On the contrary, one should endeavor to form people who are intelligent and capable enough to familiarize themselves with any area of knowledge that will become important for them. That is why the subject matter within the so-called *exact sciences* should be intensively limited, as well as the time allotted to foreign languages for children with little linguistic talent. The mind must be given adequate opportunity to exercise itself. To that end, abstract activity cannot be lacking. For that purpose, depending on talent, one should refer preferably to the classics or to mathematics. Practical exercises of mind should be placed in any case next to abstract, intellectual exercises.

Teaching girls to know and understand the world and people, and learn how to associate with them, should be considered the essential duty of the school. It has become impressively clear to us that a right relation to our fellow creatures is only possible within the framework of a right relation to the Creator.

Thus we come back to the concept that religious education is the most important component of education. The most urgent duty is to open the child's path to God. Thus we can also say that to be formed religiously one must have *living faith*. To have living faith means to know God, to love him, to serve him.

Whoever knows God (in the measure in which knowledge of God is possible through natural and supernatural light) cannot do other than love him; whoever loves him cannot do other than serve him. Thus, matters of mind and heart, achievement and act of will are living faith. He who knows how to awaken faith trains all faculties. But one can only awaken it when one also summons up all the faculties. This cannot be done through tedious intellectual instruction, but it also cannot be done through fanatic instruction which "appeals to the emotions"; on the contrary, this can be done only through a religious instruction which leads from the fullness of one's own religious life to the depths of the Godhead, an instruction which is able to present God in his kindness; such instruction enkindles love and exacts proof through deed, and it may so challenge because one achieves this by oneself. Wherever the soul is enkindled, that soul itself longs for action; and it eagerly grasps the forms of practical life for which God and Holy Church have provided: participation in the Holy Sacrifice of the Mass, a participation which consummates the holy sacrifice *as* an offering in union with the Eucharistic Lord, festive praise of God, and all works of love in which Christ is served in the members of his Mystical Body. The entire abundance of the supernatural world of the spirit is opened to the soul thereby, and an inexhaustible abundance of formative material which enters into it is thus able to build up and transform it.

—EW, 135–39

A YOUNG WIDOW PRAYS

Edith Stein's widowed mother was the main inspiration for her autobiography, Life in a Jewish Family. *The book contains many fine depictions of her family's resilience in the face of difficulties, including this vignette, which describes deep faith on the part of her cousin's grieving widow.*

His elder brother Walter [Edith's cousin] had always given his parents cause to worry.... [He] was apprenticed to a respectable business firm as far away from home and from his old influences as possible. But neither there nor in a subsequent job did he last long, for soon he was deep in debt and mixed up in all kinds of shady deals. His father sent him to America, but before long he turned up again. When the war [World War I] started, he was dispatched to the front at once. A daredevil soldier, he was almost immediately home again with an Iron Cross and a serious injury to his jaw. The old way of life began again. My uncle had no alternative but to cut off all contact with him and to forbid him entry into his paternal home.... He finally married a Christian girl with a lower middle-class background. He lived in the crowded workers' apartment which belonged to his father-in-law, a respectable cabinet-maker. Walter's parents were not happy with his misalliance and continued to ignore him and his family. But it was a good marriage, and the young wife was inconsolable when he died after a very short illness. She was left with two small children. His parents went to the funeral. On the way to the grave, his daughter-in-law clung to Uncle's arm. When the rabbi had said the final prayers and the whole group of mourners turned to leave, the young woman knelt down at the grave and, in her grief, prayed the Lord's Prayer aloud. Naturally, that was something totally unheard of in a Jewish cemetery but, instead of being offended by it, all were deeply moved. —LJF, 182, 183

DOGMA'S DOOR TO ORDINATION OPEN

The following is not the only assertion of Edith Stein about the question of women's ordination, but it demonstrates the care with which she weighed evidence from the church's storehouse of dogma.

Before considering men and women's common vocation in God's service, we would like to consider the problem of the distribution of vocations according to the natural order. Should certain positions be reserved for only men, others for only women, and perhaps a few open for both? I believe that this question also must be answered negatively. The strong individual differences existing within both sexes must be taken into account. Many women have masculine characteristics just as many men share feminine ones. Consequently, every so-called "masculine" occupation may be exercised by many women as well as many "feminine" occupations by certain men.

It seems right, therefore, that no legal barriers of any kind should exist. Rather, one can hope that a natural choice of vocation may be made thanks to an upbringing, education, and guidance in harmony with the individual's nature; unsuitable elements should be eliminated by strict objective requirements. The differences between masculine and feminine natures indicate clearly that a specific aptitude for certain professions is present in each. Thus, the choice of a profession will usually resolve itself.

Masculine vocations usually require bodily strength, the ability for predominantly abstract thought, and independent creativity: as an example, we might cite the hard physical labor required in industry, trade, and agriculture; or, to cite another example, the abstract thought required in technological fields such as mathematics and theoretical physics; and, finally, this can be seen even in the precision needed in clerical and administrative work of a mechanical nature and in certain branches of art. True feminine qualities are required wherever feeling, intuition, empathy, and adaptability come into play. Above all, this activity involves the *total person* in caring for, cultivating, helping, understanding, and in encouraging the gifts of the other. And since woman is mainly concerned with serving people and making provisions for them, she is able to function well in all educational and medical professions, in all social work, in the human sciences, in the arts which depict humanity, as well as in the business world and in public and parochial administration.

In times of extreme economic distress such as ours [1931], it would not be feasible or possible to make distinctions between masculine and feminine professions; everyone must take any employment as soon as it is offered, whether or not it suits his or her specific individual talents. Today, almost on an average, people are in "vocations" to which they are not called by nature; one can almost consider it a stroke of luck when it is otherwise. Then there is nothing left but to make the most of the situation: the pertinent professional requirements must be satisfied but not at the cost of denying one's own nature by permitting it to atrophy; rather, it should contribute to the good of one's associates. (This may mean, for example, that the woman employed even in mechanical work will prove to be sympathetic and charitable to her colleagues; and the man caught in an unsuitable job nevertheless will exhibit inventive qualities in organizing his work.) Of course, this demands a high degree of personal maturity and an unconditional good will in doing one's best in any given situation. Such a perspective can hardly be attained without understanding that the circumstances of life are God-given, that one's work is service to God, and that the gifts which God gives must be developed to his glory in this work. This is valid not only for those vocations consecrated to God but for every vocation; and yet, of course, the vocation which is designated as being consecrated to God does stand out as being especially meaningful.

In common usage we say that priests and religious must be especially *called,* which means that a particular call must be sent to them by God. Is there any difference between the call sent to man and that to woman? Women just as men have been called to the religious state at all times. And when we consider the manifold ramifications of contemporary religious life, when we acknowledge that the extremely diverse works of charity in our times are practiced also by the feminine orders and congregations, we can see only one essential difference which still exists in reality: the actual priestly work is reserved for men. This introduces us now to the difficult and much debated question of *priesthood for women.*

If we consider the attitude of the Lord himself, we understand that he accepted the free loving services of women for himself and his Apostles and that women were among his disciples and most intimate confidants. Yet he did not grant them the priesthood, not even to his mother, Queen of Apostles, who was exalted above all humanity in human perfection and fullness of grace.

In the early church, women played an active part in the various congregational charities, and their intense apostolate as confessors and martyrs had a profound effect. Virginal purity was celebrated in liturgy, and for women there was also a consecrated ecclesiastical office — the diaconate with its special ordination — but the church did not go so far as to admit them to the priesthood as well. And in later historical developments, women were displaced from these posts; also, it seems that under the influence of the Hebraic and Roman judicial concepts, there was a gradual decline in their canonical status. We are witnessing a decided change here in recent times: feminine energies are now strongly demanded as help in church charities and pastoral work. In recent militant movements, the women are demanding that their activities be recognized once more as an ordained church ministry, and it may well be that one day attention will be given to their demands. Whether this will be the first step then, finally, on the path leading to women in the priesthood is the question.

It seems to me that such an implementation by the church, until now unheard of, cannot be forbidden by *dogma*. However, the practicality of such a recommendation brings into play various arguments both pro and con. —EW, 81–84

TERESA, GREAT WOMAN

The Autobiography *of St. Teresa of Avila had a determinant influence on Edith Stein's decision to be baptized a Catholic in 1922. Later on she took the name of the first woman Doctor of the Church when she entered Teresa's order, the Discalced Carmelites. These selections concerning St. Teresa's approach to prayer are taken from a bio-historical sketch, "Love for Love," published by Sr. Teresa Benedicta soon after she entered Carmel in 1933.*

Yesterday in our monastery church we had perpetual adoration [forty hours devotion]. On such days, the faithful who are associated with our Carmel gather around the altar singing and praying from about six o'clock in the morning until about ten o'clock at night. Then the church is closed and during the night the sisters take turns keeping watch in the choir before the Blessed Sacrament. While outside in carnival's frantic tumult people get drunk and delirious, while political battles separate them, and great need depresses them so much that many forget to look to heaven, at such still places of prayer hearts are opened to the Lord. In place of the cold, the contempt, that he receives out there, they offer him their warm love. They want to atone for the insults that the divine heart must endure daily and hourly. By their steadfast supplications, they draw down God's grace and mercy on a humanity submerged in sin and need. In our time, when the powerlessness of all natural means for battling the overwhelming misery everywhere has been demonstrated so obviously, an entirely new understanding of the power of prayer, of expiation, and of vicarious atonement has again awakened. This is why people of faith crowd the places of prayer, also why, everywhere, there is a blazing demand for contemplative monasteries whose entire life is devoted to prayer and expiation. Also suddenly there is talk in all corners and parts about the silent Carmel which just a few years ago was a little known country. The desire for new foundations is surfacing in the most varied places. One almost feels transported into the time when our Holy Mother Teresa, the foundress of the reformed Carmel, traveled all over Spain from north to south and from west to east to plant new vineyards of the Lord. One would like to bring into our times also something of the spirit of this great woman who built amazingly during a century of battles and disturbances. May she herself bless this little picture of her life and works, that it may capture at least some of the radiance of her spirit and convey it to the hearts of readers. Then surely will people desire to know her better from the sources, from the rich treasure of her own works. And whoever has learned to draw from these sources will never tire of gaining courage and strength from them again and again....

In spite of all her agonizing pain, [Teresa] steadfastly continued in contemplative prayer according to the directions in her spiritual guidebook, and God rewarded this courageous fidelity by even then raising her to a high level of the interior life. In her writings, this doctor of prayer later presented the mystical life of grace in all its stages with incomparable clarity. The neophyte who was beginning to practice prayer did not yet know what was happening in her soul. But in order to make her further development intelligible, it is necessary to say a few words here about the interior life.

Prayer is the communication of the soul with God. God is love, and love is goodness giving itself away. It is a fullness of being that does not want to remain enclosed in itself, but rather to share itself with others, to give itself to them, and to make them happy. All of creation exists thanks to this divine love spending itself. However, the highest of all creatures are those endowed with spirit, able to receive God's love with understanding and to return it freely: angels and human souls. Prayer is the highest achievement of which the human spirit is capable. But it is not merely a human achievement. Prayer is a Jacob's ladder on which the human spirit ascends to God and God's grace descends to people. The stages of prayer are distinguished according to the measure in which the natural efforts of the soul and God's grace participate. When the soul is no longer active by virtue of its own efforts, but is simply a receptacle for grace, one speaks of a mystical life of prayer.

So-called vocal prayer is designated as the lowest stage, prayer that remains within specifically designated spoken forms: the Our Father, the Hail Mary, the rosary, the Divine Office. Of course, "vocal" prayer is not to be understood as simply saying words. If the mere words of a prayer alone are said without the soul's raising itself to God, this is only an outward show and not real prayer. The designated words, however, support the spirit and prescribe to it a fixed path.

Meditative prayer is one stage higher. Here the spirit moves more freely without being bound to specific words. It immerses itself, for example, in the mystery of the birth of Jesus. The spirit's imagination transports it to the grotto in Bethlehem, seeing the child in the manger, the holy parents, the shepherds, and the kings. The intellect ponders the greatness of divine mercy, the emotions are seized by love and thankfulness, the will decides to make itself more worthy of divine love. This is how meditative prayer involves all the soul's powers and, when practiced with faithful persistence, can gradually remake the whole person. However, the Lord has yet another way of rewarding fidelity in meditation: by elevation to a higher manner of praying.

St. Teresa calls the next stage the prayer of quiet or of simplicity. Various activities are replaced by a recollection of spiritual energies. The soul is no longer in the position to reflect intellectually or to make definite decisions; she is completely engaged by something that she cannot avoid, the presence of her God who is close to her and allows her to rest in him. While the lower prayer stages are accessible to every believer by human effort, albeit aided by the grace of God, we are now standing at the border of the mystical life of grace that cannot be entered by virtue of human energy, for here only God's special favor grants admission.

If the perception of God's presence is already something which totally captivates the soul and gives it a happiness incomparable to any earthly happiness, then this is greatly surpassed by the union with the Lord, which, at first, is usually granted to it for only a very short time.

At this stage of mystical favor many events occur that are also outwardly recognized as extraordinary: ecstasies and visions. The energy of the soul is so attracted by the supernatural influence that its lower faculties, the senses, lose their effectiveness entirely. The soul no longer sees or hears anything, the body no longer feels pain when injured, in some cases becomes rigid like someone dead. But the soul lives an intensified life as if it were outside of its body. Sometimes the Lord himself appears to it in bodily form, sometimes the Mother of God or an angel or saint. It sees these heavenly forms as if through bodily perception, or also in imagination. Or its intellect is supernaturally enlightened and gains insight into hidden truths. Such private revelations usually have the purpose of teaching souls about their own condition or that of others, of confiding God's intentions to them, and of forming them for a specific task for which

God has selected them. They are seldom absent in the lives of saints, though they by no means belong to the essence of holiness. Usually they only appear during a certain phase and later vanish again.

These souls, which have been sufficiently prepared and tested by repeated transitory union with him, by extraordinary illuminations, and at the same time through suffering and various trials, the Lord wishes to bind to himself permanently. He enters into a covenant with them that is called "spiritual betrothal." He expects them to put themselves completely at his service; at the same time, he takes them into safekeeping, cares for them, and is always ready to grant their requests.

Finally, Teresa calls the highest stage of blessedness "spiritual marriage." The extraordinary events have now stopped, but the soul is constantly united with the Lord. She enjoys his presence even in the midst of external activities without being hindered in the least. The saint had to go through all of these stages during a development that took years before she could account for them herself and give others advice....

The wondrous events that occurred at the saint's burial, the incorrupt state of her body that was determined by repeated disinterments, the numerous miracles that she worked during her life and then really in earnest after her death, the enthusiastic devotion of the entire Spanish people for their saint—all of this led to the initiation of the investigations preparatory to her canonization, already in the year 1595. Paul V declared her blessed in a brief on April 24, 1614. Her canonization by Gregory XV followed on March 22, 1622. Her feast day was designated as October 15, because the ten days after her death were dropped (October 5–14, 1582) due to the Gregorian calendar reform.

Luis de León said of Teresa: "I neither saw nor knew the saint during her lifetime. But today, albeit she is in heaven, I know her and see her in her two living reflections, that is, in her daughters and in her writings." Actually, there are few saints as humanly near to us as our Holy Mother. Her writings, which she penned as they came to her, in obedience to the order of her confessor, wedged between all of her burdens and work, serve as classical masterpieces of Spanish literature. In incomparably clear, simple, and sincere language they tell of the wonders of grace that God worked in a chosen soul. They tell of the indefatigable efforts of a woman with the daring and strength of a man, revealing natural intelligence and heavenly wisdom, a deep knowledge of human nature and a rich spirit's innate sense of humor, the infinite love of a heart tender as a bride's and kind as a mother's. The great family of religious that she founded, all who have been given the enormous grace of being called her sons and daughters, look up with thankful love to their Holy Mother and have no other desire than to be filled by her spirit, to walk hand in hand with her the way of perfection to its goal.

—HL, 29; 38–40; 65–66

MARY'S SYMBOLIC VALUE

Mary, the Mother of Jesus, always occupied a place of choice in Edith Stein's spiritual vision of discipleship: she was a special model for women and girls, and her patronage as Queen of Carmel drew Edith to the Carmelites when she decided to enter religious life.

Mary is the most perfect symbol of the church because she is its prefigurement and origin. She is also a unique organ of the church, that organ from which the entire Mystical Body, even the Head itself, was formed. She might be called, and happily so, the heart of the church in order to indicate her central and vital position in it. The terms *body, head,* and *heart* are of course simply metaphors. But their meaning, nevertheless, is somehow absolutely real. There is a distinctive coherence between head and heart, and they certainly play an essential role in the human body; all other organs and limbs are dependent on them for their existence and function. Just as certainly, through her unique relation with Christ, Mary must have a real — that means here a mystic — relationship with the other members of the church. This relationship extends far above that of the other members in intensity, nature, and importance; it is analogous to the relationship which a mother has with her children, a relationship surpassing that which the children have among themselves. The title of Mary as our mother is not merely symbolic. Mary is our mother in the most real and lofty sense, a sense which surpasses that of earthly maternity. She begot our life of grace for us because she offered up her entire being, body and soul, as the Mother of God.

That is why an intimate bond exists between Mary and ourselves. She loves us, she knows us, she exerts herself to bring each one of us into the closest possible relationship with the Lord — that which we are above all supposed to be. Of course, this is true for all humanity, but most particularly for women. The maternity and bridehood of the *Virgo-Mater* is continued, so to speak, in their maternity, natural and supernatural, and in their life as brides of Christ. And just as the heart sustains the other organs of woman's body and makes it possible for them to function, so we may genuinely believe there is just such a collaboration of Mary with every woman wherever that woman is fulfilling her vocation as woman; just so, there is a collaboration of Mary with us in all works of the church. But just as grace cannot achieve its work in souls unless they open themselves to it in free decision, so also Mary cannot function fully as a mother if people do not entrust themselves to her. Those women who wish to fulfill their feminine vocations in one of several ways will most surely succeed in their goals if they not only keep the ideal of the *Virgo-Mater* before their eyes and strive to form themselves according to her image, but if they also entrust themselves to her guidance and place themselves completely under her care. She herself can form in her own image those who belong to her. — EW, 240–41

5

Freedom at the Cross

✝

Long before she became a Christian the cross was a prevalent symbol in Edith's cultural surroundings. She was born in Silesia, a part of Germany where churches, chapels, and roadside shrines displaying Jesus on the cross are a familiar sight. In her autobiography she recorded the impression left on her by a hillside across from Göttingen's Nicolausberg with its "three windswept trees which always reminded me of the three crosses on Golgotha."

But eventually the prominence of the cross went beyond stark symbolism. An important occasion in her conversion was a visit she paid to Anna Reinach, the widow of Adolph Reinach, one of Husserl's trusted collaborators who had recently died in World War I. In witnessing the deep consolation that the widow drew from her Christian faith Edith was convinced she had met the power of the cross, and she found the encounter melting the barriers of disbelief within her.

She eventually asserted in her own way that the cross could be an eminently positive influence on a person's life when she asked to have the cross as her "subtitle" upon entering the Carmelites. She would be known as Sister Teresa Benedicta of the Cross. Years later she ratified this decision by assuring a friend in a letter that "one cannot wish for a deliverance from the cross when one bears the noble title 'of the Cross.'"

In her lengthy, synthetic work Finite and Eternal Being *she expounds on how embracing the cross is a matter of letting God guide us through the dark night of suffering to the light of the resurrection. For her, the cross is not a dead-end but a doorway to solidarity with those who suffer: "You can be at all fronts, wherever there is grief, in the power of the cross. Your compassionate love takes you everywhere, this love from the divine heart" (see selection "Elevation of the Cross").*

EVENTUALLY GOLGOTHA

For Edith Stein the cross is a "mystery" and an all-embracing spiritual instrument of God's purification. Christians should lend all life's moments to its transforming power.

"Thy will be done," in its full extent, must be the guideline for the Christian life. It must regulate the day from morning to evening, the course of the year and the entire life. Only then will it be the sole concern of the Christian. All other concerns the Lord takes over. This one alone, however, remains ours as long as we live.... And, sooner or later, we begin to realize this. In the childhood of the spiritual life, when we have just begun to allow ourselves to be directed by God, then we feel his guiding hand quite firmly and surely. But it doesn't always stay that way. Whoever belongs to Christ, must go the whole way with him. He must mature to adulthood: he must one day or other walk the way of the cross to Gethsemane and Golgotha.

—MC, 14–15

"THE CROSS HAS NO PURPOSE OF ITSELF"

Since Christ died "in order to give us life," our dying to self is oriented toward life. The cross for us is then a means, not an end in itself. Edith Stein sees it as the instrument of salvation that enables us to make "room for the spirit."

Christ took the yoke of the Law upon himself in that he fulfilled it perfectly and died for and through the Law. Just so did he free from the Law those who wished to receive life from him. But they can receive it only if they relinquish their own life. *For those who are baptized in Christ are baptized in his death.* They are submerged in his life in order to become members of his body and as such to suffer and to die with him but also to arise with him to eternal, divine life. This life will be ours in its *fullness* only on the day of glory. But even now we have — "in the flesh" — a share therein insofar as we believe: believe that Christ died for us in order to give us life. It is this faith that unites us to him as the members are joined to the head and opens for us the stream of his life. And so faith in the Crucified — a living faith joined to loving surrender — is for us entrance into life and the beginning of future glory. Therefore the cross is our only claim to glory: *Far be it from me to glory except in the cross of our Lord Jesus Christ, by which the world has been crucified to me, and I to the world.* He who has decided for Christ is dead to the world and the world to him. He carries *in his body the marks of the Lord's wounds,* is weak and despised by the people but is precisely therefore strong because *the power of God is mighty in the weak.* Knowing this, Jesus' disciple not only takes up the cross that is laid upon him but he also crucifies himself: *Those who belong to Christ Jesus have crucified the flesh with its passions and desires.* They have waged an unrelenting battle against their nature, that the life of sin might die in them and room be made for the life of the spirit. That last is what is important. The cross has no purpose of itself. It rises on high and points above. But it is not merely a sign — it is Christ's powerful weapon; the shepherd's staff with which the divine David moves against the hellish Goliath; with it he strikes mightily against heaven's gate and throws it wide open. Then streams of divine light flow forth and enfold all who are followers of the Crucified. —SC, 15–16

TO STAND AT THE CROSS

This poem was written on Good Friday in the troubled year of 1938. It stresses the "cost of discipleship" and regards a willingness to share in Christ's suffering as a precondition to a share in his glory.

Juxta Crucem Tecum Stare

Today I stood with you beneath the cross,
And felt more clearly than I ever did
That you became our Mother only there.
Even an earthly mother faithfully
Seeks to fulfill the last will of her son.
But you became the handmaid of the Lord.
The life and being of the God made Man
Was perfectly inscribed in your own life.
So you could take your own into your heart,
And with the lifeblood of your bitter pains
You purchased life anew for every soul.
You know us all, our wounds, our imperfections;
But you also know the celestial radiance
Which your Son's love would shed on us in heaven.
Thus carefully you guide our faltering footsteps,
No price too high for you to lead us to our goal.
But those whom you have chosen for companions
To stand with you around the eternal throne,
They here must stand with you beneath the cross,
And with the lifeblood of their own bitter pains
Must purchase heavenly glory for those souls
Whom God's own Son entrusted to their care.

—from CC, 423–24

LOVE OF THE CROSS: THOUGHTS FOR JOHN OF THE CROSS

St. John of the Cross, with his demanding doctrine of nada *and* todo *[nothing and all], is the subject of the following reflection. According to the editors of her published works Sr. Teresa Benedicta probably wrote it at Cologne for the feast of the "Doctor Mysticus" on November 24, 1934.*

We hear repeatedly that St. John of the Cross desired nothing for himself but to suffer and be despised. We want to know the reason for this love of suffering. Is it merely the loving remembrance of the path of suffering of our Lord on earth, a tender impulse to be humanly close to him by a life resembling his? This does not seem to correspond to the lofty and strict spirituality of the mystical teacher. And in relation to the Man of Sorrows, it would almost seem that the victoriously enthroned king, the divine conqueror of sin, death, and hell is forgotten. Did not Christ lead captivity captive? Has he not transported us into a kingdom of light and called us to be happy children of our heavenly Father?

The sight of the world in which we live, the need and misery, and an abyss of human malice, again and again dampens jubilation over the victory of light. The world is still deluged by mire, and still but a small flock has escaped from it to the highest mountain peaks. The battle between Christ and the Antichrist is not yet over. The followers of Christ have their place in this battle, and their chief weapon is the cross.

What does this mean? The burden of the cross that Christ assumed is that of corrupted human nature, with all its consequences in sin and suffering to which fallen humanity is subject. The meaning of the way of the cross is to carry this burden out of the world. The restoration of freed humanity to the heart of the heavenly Father, taking on the status of a child, is the free gift of grace, of merciful love. But this may not occur at the expense of divine holiness and justice. The entire sum of human failures from the first Fall up to the Day of Judgment must be blotted out by a corresponding measure of expiation. The way of the cross is this expiation. The triple collapse under the burden of the cross corresponds to the triple fall of humanity: the first sin, the rejection of the Savior by his chosen people, the falling away of those who bear the name of Christian.

The Savior is not alone on the way of the cross. Not only are there adversaries around him who oppress him, but also people who succor him. The archetype of followers of the cross for all time is the Mother of God. Typical of those who submit to the suffering inflicted on them and experience his blessing by bearing it is Simon of Cyrene. Representative of those who love him and yearn to serve the Lord is Veronica. Everyone who, in the course of time, has borne an onerous destiny in remembrance of the suffering Savior or who has freely taken up works of expiation has by doing so canceled some of the mighty load of human sin and has helped the Lord carry his burden. Or rather, Christ the head effects expiation in these members of his Mystical Body who put themselves, body and soul, at his disposal for carrying out his work of salvation. We can assume that the prospect of the faithful who would follow him on his way of the cross strengthened the Savior during his night on the Mount of Olives. And the strength of these cross-bearers helps him after each of his falls. The righteous under the Old Covenant accompany him on the stretch of the way from the first to the second collapse. The disciples, both men and women, who surrounded him during his earthly life, assist him on the second stretch. The lovers of the cross, whom he has awakened and will always continue to awaken anew in the changeable history of the struggling church, these are his allies at the end of time. We, too, are called for that purpose.

Thus, when someone desires to suffer, it is not merely a pious reminder of the suffering of the Lord. Voluntary expiatory suffering is what truly and really unites one to the Lord intimately.

When it arises, it comes from an already existing relationship with Christ. For, by nature, a person flees from suffering. And the mania for suffering caused by a perverse lust for pain differs completely from the desire to suffer in expiation. Such lust is not a spiritual striving, but a sensory longing, no better than other sensory desires, in fact worse, because it is contrary to nature. Only someone whose spiritual eyes have been opened to the supernatural correlations of worldly events can desire suffering in expiation, and this is only possible for people in whom the spirit of Christ dwells, who as members [*Glieder*] are given life by the Lord, receive his power, his meaning, and his direction. Conversely, works of expiation bind one closer to Christ, as every community that works together on one task becomes more and more closely knit and as the limbs [*Glieder*] of a body, working together organically, continually become more strongly one.

But because being one with Christ is our sanctity, and progressively becoming one with him our happiness on earth, the love of the cross in no way contradicts being a joyful child of God. Helping Christ carry his cross fills one with a strong and pure joy, and those who may and can do so, the builders of God's kingdom, are the most authentic children of God. And so those who have a predilection for the way of the cross by no means deny that Good Friday is past and that the work of salvation has been accomplished. Only those who are saved, only children of grace, can in fact be bearers of Christ's cross. Only in union with the divine Head does human suffering take on expiatory power. To suffer and to be happy although suffering, to have one's feet on the earth, to walk on the dirty and rough paths of this earth and yet to be enthroned with Christ at the Father's right hand, to laugh and cry with the children of this world and ceaselessly to sing the praises of God with the choirs of angels, this is the life of the Christian until the morning of eternity breaks forth. —HL, 91–93

ELEVATION OF THE CROSS
September 14, 1939

This and the following two texts are exhortations that Edith Stein gave at the invitation of her prioress (in 1939, 1940, and 1941), to introduce the community of nuns to the paraliturgical ceremony of renewal of their monastic vows. As stipulated in their Rule, Carmelite nuns each year renew their vows on the feast of the Exaltation of the Cross on September 14 and begin the long fast until Easter.

"Hail, cross, our only hope!" This is what the holy church summoned us to exclaim during the time for contemplating the bitter suffering of our Lord Jesus Christ. The jubilant exclamation of the Easter Alleluia silenced the serious song of the cross. But the sign of our salvation greeted us amid the time of Easter joy, since we were recalling the discovery of the one who had passed from sight. At the end of the cycle of ecclesiastical feasts, the cross greets us through the heart of the Savior. And now, as the church year draws toward an end, it is raised high before us and is to hold us spellbound, until the Easter Alleluia summons us anew to forget the earth for a while and to rejoice in the marriage of the Lamb.

Our holy order has us begin our fast with the Exaltation of the Holy Cross. And it leads us to the foot of the cross to renew our holy vows. The Crucified One looks down on us and asks us whether we are still willing to honor what we promised in an hour of grace. And he certainly has reason to ask. More than ever the cross is a sign of contradiction. The followers of the Antichrist show it far more dishonor than did the Persians who stole it. They desecrate the images of the cross, and they make every effort to tear the cross out of the hearts of Christians. All too often they have succeeded even with those who, like us, once vowed to bear Christ's cross after him. Therefore, the Savior today looks at us, solemnly probing us, and asks each one of us: Will you remain faithful to the Crucified? Consider carefully! The world is in flames, the battle between Christ and the Antichrist has broken into the open. If you decide for Christ, it could cost you your life. Carefully consider what you promise. Taking and renewing vows is a dreadfully serious business. You make a promise to the Lord of heaven and earth. If you are not deadly serious about your will to fulfill it, you fall into the hands of the living God.

Before you hangs the Savior on the cross, because he became *obedient* to death on the cross. He came into the world not to do his own will, but his Father's will. If you intend to be the bride of the Crucified, you too must completely renounce your own will and no longer have any desire except to fulfill God's will. He speaks to you in the holy rule and the constitutions of the order. He speaks to you through the mouth of your superiors. He speaks to you by the gentle breath of the Holy Spirit in the depths of your heart. To remain true to your vow of obedience, you must listen to this voice day and night and follow its orders. However, this means daily and hourly crucifying your self-will and self-love.

The Savior hangs naked and destitute before you on the cross because he has chosen *poverty.* Those who want to follow him must renounce all earthly goods. It is not enough that you once left everything out there and came to the monastery. You must be serious about it now as well. Gratefully receive what God's providence sends you. Joyfully do without what he may let you to do without. Do not be concerned with your own body, with its trivial necessities and inclinations, but leave concern to those who are entrusted with it. Do not be concerned about the coming day and the coming meal.

The Savior hangs before you with a pierced heart. He has spilled his heart's blood to win your heart. If you want to follow him in holy *purity,* your heart must be free of every earthly desire. Jesus, the Crucified, is to be the only object of your longings, your wishes, your thoughts.

Are you now alarmed by the immensity of what the holy vows require of you? You need not be alarmed. What you have promised is indeed beyond your own weak, human power. But it is not beyond the power of the Almighty — this power will become yours if you entrust yourself to him, if he accepts your pledge of troth. He does so on the day of your holy profession and will do it anew today. It is the loving heart of your Savior that invites you to follow. It demands your obedience because the human will is blind and weak. It cannot find the way until it surrenders itself entirely to the divine will. He demands poverty because hands must be empty of earth's goods to receive the goods of heaven. He demands chastity because only the heart detached from all earthly love is free for the love of God. The arms of the Crucified are spread out to draw you to his heart. He wants your life in order to give you his.

The world is in flames. The conflagration can also reach our house. But high above all flames towers the cross. They cannot consume it. It is the path from earth to heaven. It will lift one who embraces it in faith, love, and hope into the bosom of the Trinity.

The world is in flames. Are you impelled to put them out? Look at the cross. From the open heart gushes the blood of the Savior. This extinguishes the flames of hell. Make your heart free by the faithful fulfillment of your vows; then the flood of divine love will be poured into your heart until it overflows and becomes fruitful to all the ends of the earth. Do you hear the groans of the wounded on the battlefields in the west and the east? You are not a physician and not a nurse and cannot bind up the wounds. You are enclosed in a cell and cannot get to them. Do you hear the anguish of the dying? You would like to be a priest and comfort them. Does the lament of the widows and orphans distress you? You would like to be an angel of mercy and help them. Look at the Crucified. If you are nuptially bound to him by the faithful observance of your holy vows, your *being* is precious blood. Bound to him, you are omnipresent as he is. You cannot help here or there like the physician, the nurse, the priest. You can be at all fronts, wherever there is grief, in the power of the cross. Your compassionate love takes you everywhere, this love from the divine heart. Its precious blood is poured everywhere soothing, healing, saving.

The eyes of the Crucified look down on you asking, probing. Will you make your covenant with the Crucified anew in all seriousness? What will you answer him? "Lord, where shall we go? You have the words of eternal life." *Ave Crux, Spes unica!*

—HL, 94–96

THE MARRIAGE OF THE LAMB
September 14, 1940

Sr. Teresa Benedicta was born on Yom Kippur, the Jewish Day of Atonement. In the following passage she compares the sacrificial animals for the Day of Atonement with the Apocalypse's mystical lamb.

Venerunt nuptiae Agni et uxor eius praeparavit se (Rev. 19:7). "The marriage of the Lamb has come and his Bride has prepared herself." This is certainly what echoed in our hearts on the eve of our holy profession and should be echoing again as we solemnly renew our holy vows. Mysterious words that conceal the deeply mysterious meaning of our holy vocation. Who is the Lamb? Who is the Bride? And what kind of marriage supper is this?

"And between the throne and the four living creatures and among the elders, I saw a Lamb standing, as though it had been slain" (Rev. 5:6). When the seer of Patmos had this vision, the unforgettable day on the Jordan when John the Baptist showed him the "Lamb of God" who "takes away the sins of the world" (John 1:29) was still fresh in his memory. At that time, he had understood the word and now he understood the image. He who had once walked along the Jordan and who now appeared to him in white raiment with flaming eyes and with a judge's sword, the "first and the last" (Rev. 1:17) — he had in truth accomplished what the rites of the Old Covenant had suggested symbolically. When on the most momentous and holiest day of the year the high priest entered the Holy of Holies, into the supremely holy place of God's presence, he had previously taken two goats from the people: one on which to lay the people's sins, which were then carried out into the wilderness; the other to sprinkle its blood on the tent and ark of the covenant (Lev. 16). This was the sin offering for the people. In addition, he had to provide a young bullock for himself and his house as a sin offering and a ram as a burnt offering. He also had to sprinkle the throne of grace with the blood of the bullock. When he had prayed, unseen by human eyes, for himself and his house and for all the people of Israel, he came out to the waiting people, and sprinkled the outer altar to cleanse it from his sins and those of the people. Then he sent the living goat into the wilderness, brought forward his own burnt offering and that of the people, and had the rest of the sin offering burned before the camp (and later before the gates). The Day of Atonement was a monumental and holy day. People remained in the holy place praying and fasting. And in the evening when everything had been accomplished, there was peace and joy in their hearts because God had taken away the burden of sin and given grace.

But what had effected the reconciliation? Not the blood of the slaughtered animals and not the high priest of Aaron's descent — St. Paul made this so compellingly clear in his letter to the Hebrews — but rather the real sacrifice of reconciliation which was anticipated in all these legally prescribed sacrifices, and the high priest after the order of Melchizedek, who was represented by the priests of Aaron's line. He was also the true Passover Lamb for whose sake the angel of death passed over the houses of the Hebrews when he slew the Egyptians. The Lord himself made the disciples understand this when he ate the lamb of sacrifice with them for the last time and then gave himself to them as food.

But why did he choose the lamb as the preferred symbol? Why did he continue to reveal himself in this form on the eternal throne of glory? Because he was innocent as a lamb and meek as a lamb; and because he came in order to allow himself to be led as a lamb to the slaughter (Isa. 53:7). This, too, John had witnessed when the Lord permitted himself to be bound at the Mount of Olives and nailed to the cross at Golgotha. There on Golgotha the true sacrifice of reconciliation was accomplished. Thereby the old sacrifices lost their efficacy; and soon they ceased entirely, as did also the old priesthood when the temple was destroyed. John had witnessed all of this. Therefore, he was not surprised at the Lamb on the throne. And because he was a faithful witness to the Lamb, the Bride of the Lamb was also shown to him.

He saw "the holy city, the new Jerusalem, descending out of heaven from God, prepared like a bride adorned for her husband" (Rev. 21:2 and 9ff.). As Christ himself descended to earth from heaven, so too his Bride, the holy church, originated in heaven. She is born of the grace of God, indeed descended with the Son of God himself; she is inextricably bound to him. She is built of living stones; her cornerstone was laid when the Word of God assumed our human nature in the womb of the Virgin. At that time there was woven between the soul of the divine Child and the soul of the Virgin Mother the bond of the most intimate unity which we call betrothal.

Hidden from the entire world, the heavenly Jerusalem had descended to earth. From this first joining in betrothal, there had to be born all the living building blocks to be used for the mighty structure: each individual soul awakened to life through grace. The Bridal Mother was to become the mother of all the redeemed. Like a spore from which new cells stream continually, she was to build up the living city of God. This hidden mystery was revealed to St. John as he stood beneath the cross with the Virgin Mother and was given over to her as her son. It was then that the church came into existence visibly; her hour had come, but not yet her perfection. She lives, she is wedded to the Lamb, but the hour of the solemn marriage supper will only arrive when the dragon has been completely conquered and the last of the redeemed have fought their battle to the end.

Just as the Lamb had to be killed to be raised upon the throne of glory, so the path to glory leads through suffering and the cross for everyone chosen to attend the marriage supper of the Lamb. All who want to be married to the Lamb must allow themselves to be fastened to the cross with him. Everyone marked by the blood of the Lamb is called to this, and that means all the baptized. But not everyone understands the call and follows it. There is a call to following more closely that resounds more urgently in the soul and demands a clear answer. This is the vocation to the religious life, and the answer is the religious vows.

For the person whom the Savior calls away from all natural ties from one's family, one's people, and occupational circles to cling to him alone, the bridal connection with the Savior also becomes more prominent than for the general host of the redeemed. They want to belong preeminently to the Lamb for all eternity, to follow him wherever he goes, and to sing the song of the virgins that no one else can sing (Rev. 14:1–5).

When the attraction to religious life awakens in the soul, it is as if the Lord were courting it. And if she consecrates herself to him by profession of the vows and harkens to the *Veni, sponsa Christi!* ["Come, spouse of Christ!"], it is like an anticipation of the heavenly marriage feast. Nevertheless, this is but a prospect of the eternal feast of joy. The bridal happiness and fidelity of the soul consecrated to God must stand the test in open and hidden battles and in the everyday flow of religious life. The spouse whom she chooses is the Lamb that was killed. If she is to enter into heavenly glory with him, she must allow herself to be fastened to his cross. The three vows are the nails. The more willingly she stretches herself out on the cross and endures the blows of the hammer, the more deeply will she experience the reality of her union with the Crucified. Then being crucified itself becomes for her the marriage feast.

The vow of poverty opens one's hands so that they let go of everything they were clutching. It fastens them securely so they can no longer reach toward the things of this world. It should also bind the hands of the spirit and the soul: the desires, which again and again reach for pleasures and things; the cares that want to secure earthly life in every respect; busyness about many things which endangers the one thing necessary. Living in superfluity and secure comfort contradicts the spirit of holy poverty and separates us from the poor Crucified One. Our sisters in the early times of the reform considered themselves happy when they lacked necessities. When the difficulties had been surmounted and enough of everything was at their disposal, they feared that the Lord had withdrawn from them. There is something wrong in a monastic community when concerns for the outer life take up so much time and energy that the spiritual life suffers. And there is something wrong in the soul of the individual religious who starts to take care of herself and to go after what she wants and likes instead of abandoning herself to divine providence and gratefully receiving what it gives her through the hands of the sisters in charge. Naturally, one should, after conscientious consideration, let the superior know what one's health requires. But having done that, one is relieved of further concern. The vow of holy poverty is intended to make us as carefree as the sparrows and the lilies so that our spirits and hearts may be free for God.

Holy obedience binds our feet so that they no longer go their own way, but God's way. Children of the world say they are free when they are not subject to another's will, when no one stops them from satisfying their wishes and inclinations. For this dream of freedom, they engage in bloody battles and sacrifice life and limb. The children of God see freedom as something else. They want to be unhindered in following the Spirit of God; and they know that the greatest hindrances do not come from without, but lie within us ourselves. Human reason and will, which would like so much to be their own masters, are unaware of their susceptibility to be swayed by natural inclinations and so to be enslaved by them. There is no better way of being freed of this slavery and receptive to the guidance of the Holy Spirit than that of holy obedience. In the poem of Goethe most informed by the Christian spirit, he has his heroine say, "Obedient, my soul felt free indeed." Genuine obedience is not content merely to avoid manifestly overstepping the prescriptions of rule and constitutions or the precepts of the superiors. It actually determines to deny one's own will. Therefore, the obedient person studies the rule and the constitutions, not to ferret out how many so-called "freedoms" are still permitted, but to recognize more and more how many small sacrifices are available daily and hourly as opportunities to advance in self-denial. Such a one takes them on as an easy yoke and a light burden, because doing so deepens the conviction of being closely bound to the Lord who was obedient to death on the cross. To the children of this world such action probably appears as useless, senseless, and petty. The Savior, who for thirty years filled his daily work with such small sacrifices, will judge differently.

The vow of chastity intends to release human beings from all the bonds of natural common life, to fasten them to the cross high above all the bustle, and to free their hearts for union with the Crucified. This sacrifice, too, is not accomplished once and for all. Of course, one is cut off, externally, from occasions that can become temptations outside, but often much that distracts the spirit and the heart, robbing them of their freedom, cleaves to the memory and fantasy. Besides, there is also a danger that new ties establish themselves within the protective cloister walls and hinder full union with the Divine Heart. When we enter the order, we again become members of a family. We are to see and respect, as head and members of the Mystical Body of Christ, our superiors and the other sisters. But we are human, and something all too human can easily become mingled with holy, childlike, and sisterly love. We believe we see Christ in the people we look up to and fail to notice that we attach ourselves to them humanly and are in danger of losing sight of Christ. But human attraction is not the only cloud on purity of heart. Too little love is a worse offense against the Divine Heart than too much. Every aversion, any anger and resentment that we tolerate in our hearts, closes the door to the Savior. Involuntary stirrings naturally arise through no fault of our own, but as soon as we become aware of them, we must relentlessly oppose them. Otherwise we resist God who is love and do the devil's work. The song sung by the virgins attending the Lamb is surely one of purest love.

The cross is again raised before us. It is the sign of contradiction. The Crucified looks down on us: "Are you also going to abandon me?" The day for the renewal of vows should always be one of serious self-examination. Have we lived up to the promises made in our first fervor? Have we lived in a manner befitting brides of the Crucified, the Lamb that was slain? In the last few months one has often heard the complaint that the many prayers for peace are still without effect. What right have we to be heard? Our desire for peace is undoubtedly genuine and sincere. But does it come from a completely purified heart? Have we truly prayed "in the name of Jesus," i.e., not just with the name of Jesus on our lips, but with the spirit and in the mind of Jesus, for the glory of the Father alone, without any self-seeking? The day on which God has unrestricted power over our hearts we shall also have unrestricted power over his. If we ponder this, we will no longer dare to judge anyone else. But neither will we be discouraged if, after living in the order for a long time, we must admit we are still bunglers and beginners. The fountain from the heart of the Lamb has not dried up. We can wash our robes clean in it even today as the thief on Golgotha once did. Trusting in the atoning power of this holy fountain, we prostrate ourselves before the throne of the Lamb and answer his question: "Lord, to whom shall we go? You have the words of eternal life" (John 6:68). Let us draw from the springs of salvation for ourselves and for the entire parched world. Give us the grace to speak the bride's words with a pure heart: Come! Come, Lord Jesus. Come soon! —HL, 97–101

EXALTATION OF THE CROSS
September 14, 1941

A reference to St. Benedict and his Rule occurs at the very beginning of this selection. Sr. Teresa Benedicta pays a small tribute to the saint who founded the order she depended on for spiritual formation and accompaniment in the years between her baptism and her entry to Carmel.

In his *Holy Rule* St. Benedict ordained that the fasts for religious begin with the feast of the Exaltation of the Cross. The long-extended Easter joy and the solemn feasts of summer culminating in the crowning of the Queen of Heaven could possibly cause the image of the Crucified to fade in us or to recede, as it remained hidden during the first centuries of Christianity. But when its time came, the cross appeared gleaming in the heavens, prompting the search for the buried and forgotten wood of humiliation that was to be recognized as the sign of salvation, the emblem of faith, and the mark of the faithful. Every year, when the church again raises it before us, we are to recall the challenge of the Lord: Anyone who would follow me must take up his [or her] cross . . . ! To take up one's cross means to go the way of penance and renunciation. For us religious, to follow the Savior means to allow ourselves to be fastened to the cross by the three nails of the holy vows. The Exaltation of the Cross and the renewal of vows belong together.

The Savior has preceded us on the way of poverty. All the goods in heaven and on earth belonged to him. They presented no danger to him; he could use them and yet keep his heart completely free of them. But he knew that it is scarcely possible for people to have possessions without succumbing to them and being enslaved by them. Therefore, he gave up everything and showed more by his example than by his counsel that only one who possesses nothing possesses everything. His birth in a stable, his flight to Egypt, already indicated that the Son of Man was to have no place to lay his head. Whoever follows him must know that we have no lasting dwelling here. The more deeply we feel this, the more zealous we are in striving for the future, and we rejoice at the thought that our citizenship is in heaven. Today it is good to reflect on the fact that poverty also includes the readiness to leave our beloved monastery itself. We have pledged ourselves to enclosure and do so anew when we renew our vows. But God did not pledge to leave us within the walls of the enclosure forever. He need not do so because he has other walls to protect us. This is similar to what he does in the sacraments. For us they are the prescribed means to grace, and we cannot receive them eagerly enough. But God is not bound to them. At the moment when some external force were to cut us off from receiving the sacraments, he could compensate us, superabundantly, in some other way; and he will do so all the more certainly and generously the more faithfully we have adhered to the sacraments previously. So it is also our holy duty to be as conscientious as possible in observing the precept of enclosure, to lead without hindrance a life hidden with Christ in God. If we are faithful and are then driven out into the street, the Lord will send his angels to encamp themselves around us, and their invisible pinions will enclose our souls more securely than the highest and strongest walls. We do not need to wish for this to happen. We may ask that the experience be spared us, but only with the solemn and honestly intended addition: Not mine, but your will be done! The vow of holy poverty is to be renewed without reservation.

Your will be done! This was the content of the Savior's life. He came into the world to fulfill the Father's will, not only to atone for the sin of disobedience through his obedience, but also to lead people back to their destiny by the way of obedience. The created will is not destined to be free to exalt itself. It is called to come into unison with the divine will. If it freely submits itself to this unison, then it is permitted in freedom to participate in the perfection of creation. If a free creature declines this unison, it lapses into bondage. The human will continues to retain the possibility of choice, but it is constrained by creatures that pull and pressure it in directions straying from the development of the nature desired by God, and so away from the goal toward which it itself was directed by its original freedom. With the loss of this original freedom, it also loses security in making decisions. It becomes unsteady and wavering, buffeted by doubt and scruples or obdurate in its error. There is no other remedy for this than the following of Christ, the Son of Man, who not only promptly obeyed his heavenly Father, but also subjected himself to people who imposed the Father's will on him. The obedience enjoined by God releases the enslaved will from the bonds of creatures and leads it back to freedom. Thus, it is also the way to purity of heart.

No chains of slavery are stronger than those of passion. Under its burden body, soul, and spirit lose their strength and health, their clarity and beauty. Just as it is scarcely possible for one impaired by original sin to own things without clinging to them, so there is also the danger that any natural affection may degenerate into passion with all of its devastating consequences. God has provided two remedies for this: marriage and virginity. Virginity is the more radical and precisely therefore probably the easier way. But this is surely not the deepest reason why Christ set us an example of it. Marriage is already a great mystery as the symbol of the bond between Christ and the church and at the same time as its instrument. But virginity is a still deeper mystery. It is not only the symbol and instrument of bridal union with Christ and of the union's supernatural fruitfulness, but also participates in the union. It originates in the depths of the divine life and leads back to it again. The eternal Father in unconditional love has given his entire being to his Son. And just as unconditionally does the Son give himself back to the Father. The passage of the God Man through temporal life could alter nothing of this complete surrender of Person to Person. He belongs to the Father from eternity to eternity and could not give himself away to any human being. He could only incorporate the persons who wanted to give themselves to him into the unity of his Incarnate Divine Person as members of his Mystical Body and in this way bring them to the Father. This is why he came into the world. This is the divine fertility of his eternal virginity: that he can give souls supernatural life. And the fruitfulness of the virgins who follow the Lamb consists in the ability to assume the divine life in unmitigated strength and undivided surrender and, in union with the divine Head, to pass it on to other souls, so awaking new members for the Head.

Divine virginity has a characteristic aversion to sin as the contrary of divine holiness. However, this aversion to sin gives rise to an indomitable love for sinners. Christ has come to tear sinners away from sin and to restore the divine image in defiled souls. He comes as the child of sin — his genealogy and the entire history of the Old Covenant show this — and he seeks the company of sinners, so as to take all the sins of the world upon himself and carry them away to the infamous wood of the cross, which thereby precisely becomes the sign of his victory. This is precisely why virginal souls do not repulse sinners. The strength of their supernatural purity knows no fear of being sullied. The love of Christ impels them to descend into the darkest night. And no earthly maternal joy resembles the bliss of a soul permitted to enkindle the light of grace in the night of sins. The way to this is the cross. Beneath the cross the Virgin of virgins becomes the Mother of Grace. — HL, 102–4

HAIL CROSS, OUR ONLY HOPE!

St. Teresa Benedicta sent this note to her prioress, Mother Ambrosia Antonia Engelmann, to say she was at peace over the possibility of a permanent transfer ("stability") to the Echt monastery.

[presumably December 1941]

Dear Mother,

Once Y.R. [Your Reverence, monastic address] has read the letter from P[ater] H[irschmann, SJ] you will know his opinion. Now I would like to do nothing more at all about the matter of my stability. I put it in Y.R.'s hands and leave it to Y.R. whether to call on the Sisters, Pater Provincial, or our Father Bishop for a decision. I am satisfied with everything. A *scientia crucis* [knowledge of the cross] can be gained only when one comes to feel the cross radically. I have been convinced of that from the first moment and have said, from my heart: *Ave Crux, spes unica!* [Hail, cross, our only hope!]

Y.R.'s grateful child,
Benedicta

—SPL, 341

"SURRENDER IS THE HIGHEST ACT OF FREEDOM"

Edith Stein developed these thoughts between 1940 and 1942 to capture such lifelong concerns as the elements of human interiority, its motivational force for significant choices, and the spiritual dynamics of personal development as a Christian.

It is important to clarify as much as possible, spiritually and without imagery, what these spatial images express. These images are indispensable. But they are ambiguous and easily misunderstood. What approaches the soul from without belongs to the outer world and by this is meant whatever does not belong to the soul herself; as a rule, it also includes whatever does not belong to her body. For even though the body is called her exterior, it is her exterior, at one with her in the unity of one being and not as external as that which confronts her as totally strange and separate. Among these strange and separate ones, there is the difference between things which have a clearly exterior being, i.e., are spatially extended, and such as have an interior like the soul herself.

On the other hand we had to speak, in the soul herself, of an exterior and an interior. For when she is drawn outside, she does not leave herself; she is only farther away from her inmost region and with that, at the same time, devotes herself to the outer world. What approaches from outside has a certain right to claim her attention, and, depending on its weight, the value, and meaning it has in itself and for the soul, it deserves to be admitted to an appropriate depth of the soul. So it is objectively reasonable that she accepts it from there. But to do so, she is not required to sacrifice her position at a deeper level; because she is a spirit and her castle is a spiritual realm, there are totally different rules valid here than in the external sphere. When she is in the deepest and inmost region of this, her inner realm, then she rules over it completely and has the freedom to go to whatever place in it she pleases, without having to leave her place, the place of her rest. The possibility to move within oneself is based on the soul's being formed as an I. The I is that in the soul by which she possesses herself and that which moves within her as in its own space. The deepest point is at the same time the place of her freedom: the place at which she can collect her entire being and make decisions about it. Free decisions of lesser importance can, in a certain sense, also be made at a point located farther toward the outside. However, these are superficial decisions: it is a coincidence when such a decision proves to be appropriate, for only at the deepest point can one possibly measure everything against one's ultimate standards. Nor is it an irrefutably free decision, for anyone who does not have herself completely in hand cannot decide in true freedom but rather allows herself to be determined [by outside factors].

The human being is called upon to live in his inmost region and to have himself as much in hand as is possible only from that centerpoint; only from there can one rightly come to terms with the world. Only from there can he find the place in the world which has been intended for him. In all of this, he can never see through this inmost region completely. It is God's mystery which he alone can reveal to the degree that pleases him. However this inmost region has been laid in the human being's hand; he can make use of it in complete freedom but he also has the duty to guard it as a precious good entrusted to him. In the realm of spirits, it must be given great value: the angels have the task of protecting it. Evil spirits seek to gain control of it. God himself has chosen it as his dwelling. The good and evil spirits do not have free entrance into the inmost region. The good spirits are no more able, in natural ways, to read the "thoughts of the heart" than are the evil spirits, but they receive illumination from God about all they must know about the heart's secrets. Furthermore, there are spiritual ways in which the soul can make contact with the other created spirits. She can address herself to another spirit with whatever has become an interior word in her. This is how St. Thomas imagines the language of the angels with which they mutually communicate: as a purely spiritual self-offering with the intention of sharing with another what one has in oneself. In this wise, also, is the soundless cry to the guardian angel to be imagined, or an interior summoning of evil spirits. But even without our intention to share, the created spirits have a certain access to what occurs within us: not to that which is concealed in our inmost region, but probably about whatever has entered the interior regions of the soul in a perceptible form. From that point, they are also able to draw conclusions about that which may be concealed from their sight. We must assume that the angels protect the locked sanctuary with reverent awe. They desire only to bring the soul there in order for her to surrender it to God. But Satan strives to wrest into his possession that which is God's kingdom. He cannot do this by his own power, but the soul can surrender herself to him. She will not do this if she herself has entered her inmost region and come to know it as happens in divine union. For then she is so immersed in God and so secure that no temptation can approach her anymore. But how is it possible that she can hand herself over to the devil when she has not yet fully taken herself into possession as can happen only upon entrance to the inmost region? One can only think she does it by blindly grabbing hold, as it were, while she is still outside. She gives herself away without knowing what she surrenders by that. And neither can the devil break the seal on that which, still closed, has been handed to him. He can only destroy what remains forever hidden from him.

The soul has the right to make decisions that concern herself. It is the great mystery of personal freedom, before which God himself comes to a halt. He wants his sovereign authority over created spirits only as a free gift of their love. He knows the thoughts of the heart. He sees through the deepest foundations and abysses of the soul, where her own glance cannot penetrate unless God specifically grants her light to do so. But he does not want to take possession of her without her wanting it herself. Yet he does everything to achieve the free surrender of her will to his as a gift of her love in order, then, to be able to lead her to the bliss of union. That is the gospel John of the Cross has to announce and for which all his writings serve. What was said last about the structure of the soul's being, especially about the relation of freedom to her inmost region, does not come from the expositions of our holy Father St. John. It is therefore necessary to prove whether it is in harmony with his teaching and may, in fact, even serve to clarify his doctrine. (Only if this proves to be the case can this interjection be justified in this context.) At first glance, some of what has been said may well appear incompatible with certain of the saint's expositions.

Every human being is free and is confronted with decisions on a daily and hourly basis. But the inmost region of the soul is the place where God lives "all alone" as long as the soul has not reached the perfect union of love. Holy Mother Teresa calls it the seventh dwelling place, which opens for the soul only when the mystical marriage takes place. So then, is it only the soul which has arrived at the highest degree of perfection that decides in perfect freedom? Here it must be considered that the autonomous action of the soul apparently diminishes the more she nears her inmost self. And when she arrives there, God does everything in her; she no longer has anything more to do than to receive. However, it is precisely the taking-into-reception that expresses her free participation. But beyond that, freedom comes into play at a far more decisive stage: God does everything here only because the soul has totally surrendered herself to him. And this surrender is the highest act of her freedom. John himself depicts the mystical marriage as voluntary surrender of God and the soul to one another and ascribes so great a power to the soul that has arrived at this step of perfection that she has not only herself but even God at her service. For this highest stage of the personal life there is perfect agreement between the mystical doctrine of our holy parents and the view that the inmost region of the soul is the place of the most perfect freedom.

But how do matters stand with the large mass of humans who do not arrive at mystical marriage? Can they enter the inmost region and make decisions from there, or are they only capable of more or less superficial decisions? The answer is not a simple yes or no.

The structure of the soul's being — her greater and lesser depths as well as the inmost region — are hers by nature. Within that structure, again by nature, there exists a possibility of being as a basis for the I's mobility within this space. This I sets itself up now here, now there, according to the motivations which appeal to it. But it undertakes its movements from a position it prefers to occupy. This position, now, is not the same in everyone, rather, in the various types of persons it is determined typically. The one who desires sensory delights is mostly engrossed in a sensual satisfaction or preoccupied about gaining such satisfaction; his position is located very far from his inmost region. One who seeks truth lives principally at the heart of an actively searching intellect. If he is really concerned about the truth (not merely collecting single bits of knowledge) then he is perhaps nearer to the God who is Truth, and therefore to his own inmost region than he himself knows. To these two examples we wish to add only a third, which seems to have particular meaning: the "I-human being," that is, the one for whom his own I stands as the central point. Considered superficially, one might think such a human being to be particularly close to his inmost region. Yet, perhaps for no other type is the way there as obstructed as for this one. (Every human being has something of this in himself as long as he has not suffered through to the end of the Dark Night.) We must examine for all these types the possibilities for the mobility of the I, the possibilities of free decision-making, and the possibility of reaching the inmost region.

When the sensual human being, who is engrossed in some satisfaction, is presented with the possibility of procuring something even more satisfying, he will perhaps, without further consideration or choice move from satisfaction into action. A movement takes place, but not an actually free decision; nor a breakthrough to a greater depth when the drives lie on the same level. But it is possible for the sensual human being to be approached by something that belongs to a completely different area of values. No type is exclusively restricted to one area; only one area has the ascendancy over the others at a given time. He may, for example, be asked to deny himself some pleasure in order to help another human being. Here, the solution will hardly be reached without a free decision. At all events, the sensual person will not make a sacrifice as a matter of course; rather he will have to pull himself together to do so. If he declines — whether after some evaluation or with an immediate "that's out of the question" — that, too, is a decision of the will. In an extreme case one can even think of him continuing in his enjoyment without rejecting the sacrifice, there where the spirit is so suffocated in sensuality that the challenge cannot even reach him. The words are heard, and perhaps their immediate meaning may be understood, but the area where the real sense of the call would be received is buried in rubble. In this extreme, not only does a single free decision fail to materialize but freedom itself was already abandoned previously. Where one declines, the meaning is probably grasped, even though, apparently, it is not evaluated at full range. In such a refusal to take the full range into consideration lies both the superficiality of the decision and a bridled freedom. One does not allow certain motives to appeal with their full import and takes good care not to return to that depth where these motives could instigate involvement. In this case, one surrenders oneself to a single area of decision-making. One never takes oneself, i.e., all the deeper levels of one's own being, into one's hands and so deprives oneself of the possibility of taking a stand after evaluating the true circumstances, i.e., what is truly reasonable and truly free. Besides this superficial rejection, one can think of course of something that would be more appropriate: having allowed the call for help to be weighed fully by the soul, with full consideration of all the aspects, one could feel obliged to refuse when evaluation of all the pros and cons establishes it as unjustified. Such a refusal is on the same level as compliance after objectively weighing the pros and cons. Both are possible only when the sensual human being has abandoned his attitude as a sensual person and has gone over to an ethical attitude, i.e., in the position of one who wants to recognize and do what is morally right. To do this he must take up a position deep within himself: so deep, that the crossover resembles a formal transformation of the human being. And this may not even be possible in a natural way, but only on the basis of an extraordinary awakening. Yes, we may well say: an ultimately appropriate decision can be made only at the extreme depth [of the soul]. For no human being is by nature in a position to scan all the pros and cons that have a say about a decision. The decision can only be made according to one's own best knowledge and conscience, within the circumference of one's own vision. However, a person with faith knows that there is one whose view is not circumscribed but truly comprises and perceives everything. The conscience of the one who lives in this certainty of faith can no longer quiet itself by following its own best knowledge. He must strive to recognize what is right in God's eyes. (For this reason only a religious position is the truly ethical one. There is in all likelihood a natural seeking and longing for the right and good, as well as finding this in some cases, but only in seeking for the divine will can it truly reach its goal.) The one who is drawn by God himself into the soul's own inmost region and has surrendered there in the union of love, for such a one the question has been answered once and for all. Nothing further is necessary than to allow God's Spirit to direct and lead, for the Spirit will distinctly urge him on, and he will always and everywhere be certain he is doing the right thing. In that one great decision, made with the utmost freedom, all future ones are included and can then, almost as a matter of course, be made accordingly. But, instead of simply searching for the right decision in a particular case, to arrive at this height there is a long way to go — if indeed there is a way to it. One who, only here and now, seeks what is right and accordingly decides by what he believes he knows, is on the way to God and on the way to himself even when he does not know this. But he does not yet have such a hold on himself as one is given in the ultimate depth; therefore he cannot fully make disposition of himself nor can he make perfectly free decisions about things.

Whoever fundamentally seeks what is right, i.e., whoever is determined to do it always and everywhere, has made a decision about himself and has set his will within the divine will, even when it is not yet clear to him that what is right corresponds to that which God wills. But if this is not clear to him, he still lacks the secure way of discerning what is right; and he has made disposition of himself as though he had himself completely in hand, although the ultimate depth of his inmost region has not yet opened to him. The final decision only becomes possible eye to eye with God. But when one has arrived so far in the life of faith that he has committed to God completely and no longer wants anything but what God wills, has he not then arrived at his inmost region, and is [his state] still different from that of the highest union in love? It is very difficult to draw a boundary line here, and difficult, also, to know how our holy Father St. John draws it. Still I believe — objectively and as he teaches — it is necessary to acknowledge a boundary and to bring it into relief. Whoever truly wants, in blind faith, nothing more but what God wills, has, with God's grace, reached the highest state a human being can reach. His will is totally purified and free of all constraint through earthly desires; he is united to the divine will through free surrender. And still, for the highest union of love, the mystical marriage, something decisive is lacking. — SC, 142–48

TO THE RESURRECTION

In this passage from her very last work, The Science of the Cross, *Edith Stein summarizes the interplay of "faith and contemplation, death and resurrection" as expounded by St. John of the Cross. Her familiarity with biblical and liturgical renewal enriched her treatment of St. John of the Cross's teaching with insights about the full paschal mystery.*

The difference between the indwelling of God by grace and through mystical union appears to us as a fitting foundation on which to base a clear demarcation between faith and contemplation. Holy Father St. John speaks very frequently of both but he gives no actual comparison of them in a way which would enable one to make an unequivocal determination of the mutual relationship. Many times his explanations sound as though, generally speaking, there is no distinct boundary to draw; both are marked as ways to union, both as dark and loving knowledge. The darkness of faith is treated primarily in the *Ascent of Mount Carmel.* There faith is called the darkness of midnight, because we must totally renounce the light of natural knowledge in order to gain its light. John frequently gives contemplation the name used by the Areopagite [Pseudo-Dionysius], mystical theology (secret wisdom of God) and ray of darkness. The two are very close when it is said that God wraps himself in the darkness of faith when he communicates himself to the soul. On the other hand, it is precisely in these explanations in the *Ascent* that it is made clear that faith and contemplation cannot simply be synonymous since it is said that faith is the guide in the delights of pure contemplation and union. A differentiation is also prerequisite when in the foreword to the *Spiritual Canticle* it is said that mystical wisdom does not need to be understood distinctly since it resembles, in this, faith through which we love God without understanding him. Were the two to coincide there could be no talk of similarity. Difference and a close correlation are most clearly expressed, perhaps, in the passage which juxtaposes contemplation as a vague, dark, and general knowledge with clearly distinct and particular supernatural intellectual apprehensions: "The dark and general knowledge is of one kind only: contemplation which is imparted in faith."

To understand this sentence and the relation between faith and contemplation one must remember what was said in former passages about the manifold meanings necessarily covered by the word "faith"; also that contemplation can signify more than one thing. The content of divine revelation and the acceptance of this revelation are called faith; and so is the loving surrender to God about whom revelation speaks, and to whom we are indebted for [revelation]. The content of faith delivers the material for meditation: the occupation of the soul's faculties with that which we have accepted in faith, which we represent to ourselves in images, in intellectual reflection, and about which we have decided opinions. A habitual condition of loving knowledge is won as the fruit of meditation. The soul now remains in tranquil, peaceful, loving surrender in the presence of God whom she has come to know through faith without having meditated on any single article of truth. As the fruit of meditation, this is acquired contemplation. There is no difference between the content experienced here and that of faith in the third sense: the *credere in Deum,* entering into God in faith and love. But usually John of the Cross has something else in mind when he speaks of contemplation. God can grant the soul a dark, loving knowledge of himself without a preliminary practice of meditation. He can raise her suddenly into the condition of contemplation and love by infusing contemplation in her. This too does not happen without a connection to faith. As a rule it is imparted to souls who are prepared to receive it through lively faith and lives built on faith. But should ever an unbeliever be caught up by it he would, all the same, be enlightened by the hitherto rejected doctrine of faith as to the identity of the one who has seized him. And the faithful, loving soul will repeatedly take refuge from the darkness of contemplation in the sure clarity of the doctrines of faith in order to understand from that viewpoint what has happened to her. What has happened to her, however, is despite all coincidences something fundamentally other than acquired contemplation and the surrender to God in mere faith, the experience of which is similar to that of acquired contemplation. The new form is a being seized by the God whose presence is felt or — in those experiences of the Dark Night when the soul is deprived of this sensible perception of his presence — the painful wound of love and the fervent longings which remain in the soul when God withdraws from the soul. Both are mystical experiences, based on that form of indwelling which is a person-to-person touch in the inmost region of the soul. Faith, on the contrary, and all that belongs to a life of faith, rests on the indwelling by grace.

The contrast of sensibly perceived presence and sensibly perceived withdrawal of God in mystical contemplation points to something else which serves to differentiate it from faith. Faith is primarily a matter of the intellect. Though in the acceptance of faith participation of the will is expressed, it is still the acceptance of knowledge. The darkness of faith signifies a characteristic of this knowledge. Contemplation is a matter of the heart, i.e., the inmost region of the soul, and therefore of all her faculties. The presence and the apparent absence of God are felt in the heart — either in bliss or in most painful desire. Here at the inmost center where she is totally by herself, the soul, however, feels herself and her condition. As long as she is not completely purified, she feels it painfully as opposition to the experienced holiness of the God who is present there. Thus the Night of contemplation does not only designate the darkness of knowledge, but also the darkness of impurity and of purifying torment.

In faith and in contemplation the soul is taken hold of by God. The acceptance of revealed truth does not happen simply through a natural act of the will. The message of the faith comes to many who do not accept it. Natural reasons may contribute to this but there are cases in which a mysterious "cannot" is fundamental. The hour of grace has not yet come. The indwelling of faith has not yet taken place. But in contemplation the soul meets God himself, who takes possession of the soul.

God is love. Therefore, being seized by God is an enkindling in love — when the spirit is ready for it. For all that is mortal is consumed in the fire of eternal love. And that means all movements which are released in the soul through creatures. If she turns toward the creature, she withdraws herself from the divine love, although she cannot escape it. Then love becomes a fire that consumes the soul herself. The human spirit as spirit is destined for immortal being. This is shown in the immutability which he ascribes to himself in his own circumstances: he thinks that as things are ordered about him, they will forever remain. That is a deception, for during his mortal existence he is subject to change. But one hears in this the consciousness that one's being is not consumed by what is temporal, but is rooted in the eternal. According to his nature, he cannot decay like material forms. But if, in free surrender, the spirit fastens on to what is temporal he will come to feel the hand of the living God who can destroy him by his almighty power through the avenging fire of rejected divine love or can maintain him in eternal destruction like the fallen angels. This second and most actual death would be our common lot if Christ had not stepped between us and divine justice with his passion and death and opened a way for mercy.

There was nothing in Christ through his nature and his free decision that resisted love. He lived every moment of his existence in the boundless surrender to divine love. But in the Incarnation he had taken upon himself the entire burden of mankind's sin, embraced it with his merciful love, and hidden it in his soul. This he did in the *Ecce venio* ["Behold, I come"] with which he began his earthly life, and specifically renewed in his baptism, and in the *Fiat!* ["Let it be!"] of Gethsemane (Luke 22:39). This is how the expiating fire burned in his inmost being, in his entire, lifelong suffering, in the most intense form in the Garden of Olives and on the cross, because here the sensible joy of the indestructible union ceased, subjecting him totally to the Passion, and allowing this Passion to become the experience of the total abandonment by God. In the *Consummatum est* ["It is finished" (John 19:30)], the end of the expiatory fire is announced as is the final return into eternal, undisturbed union of love in the *Pater, in manus tuas commendo spiritum meum* ["Father, into your hands I commend my spirit" (Luke 23:46)].

In the Passion and death of Christ our sins were consumed by fire. If we accept that in faith, and if we accept the whole Christ in faith-filled surrender, which means, however, that we choose and walk the path of the imitation of Christ, then he will lead us "through his Passion and cross to the glory of his resurrection." This is exactly what is experienced in contemplation: passing through the expiatory flames to the bliss of the union of love. This explains its twofold character. It is death and resurrection. After the Dark Night, the Living Flame shines forth.

—SC, 161–65